# The Future of Diplomacy

# The Future of Diplomacy

Philip Seib

polity

Copyright © Philip Seib 2016

The right of Philip Seib to be identified as Author of this Work has been asserted in accordance with the UK Copyright, Designs and Patents Act 1988.

First published in 2016 by Polity Press

Polity Press
65 Bridge Street
Cambridge CB2 1UR, UK

Polity Press
350 Main Street
Malden, MA 02148, USA

ISBN-13: 978-1-5095-0719-1
ISBN-13: 978-1-5095-0720-7(pb)

A catalogue record for this book is available from the British Library.

Library of Congress Cataloging-in-Publication Data

Names: Seib, Philip M., 1949- author.
Title: The future of diplomacy / Philip Seib.
Description: Cambridge, UK ; Malden, MA : Polity Press, [2016] | Includes bibliographical references and index.
Identifiers: LCCN 2015046315 (print) | LCCN 2015049255 (ebook) | ISBN 9781509507191 (hardcover : alk. paper) | ISBN 9781509507207 (pbk. : alk. paper) | ISBN 1509507191 (hardcover : alk. paper) | ISBN 1509507205 (pbk. : alk. paper) | ISBN 9781509507221 (mobi) | ISBN 9781509507238 (epub)
Subjects: LCSH: Diplomacy.
Classification: LCC JZ1305 .S444 2016 (print) | LCC JZ1305 (ebook) | DDC 327.2--dc23
LC record available at http://lccn.loc.gov/2015046315

Typeset in 10 on 16.5pt Utopia by
Servis Filmsetting Ltd, Stockport, Cheshire
Printed and bound in the UK by CPI Group (UK) Ltd, Croydon

The publisher has used its best endeavours to ensure that the URLs for external websites referred to in this book are correct and active at the time of going to press. However, the publisher has no responsibility for the websites and can make no guarantee that a site will remain live or that the content is or will remain appropriate.

Every effort has been made to trace all copyright holders, but if any have been inadvertently overlooked the publisher will be pleased to include any necessary credits in any subsequent reprint or edition.

For further information on Polity, visit our website:
politybooks.com

# Contents

# Preface

The purpose of this short book is to stimulate thinking and conversation about the ways diplomacy is changing and what diplomacy's future is likely to hold.

Although I love diplomatic history, I have minimized historical material in the book, providing just enough to establish context as needed. Countless volumes are available that exhaustively examine where we have been. Far less has been written about where we are going. That is what interests me now.

This is a heady time to be considering such matters. Not since Gutenberg has communication changed as profoundly as has happened during the past decade or two, thanks to the internet. The latest manifestation of this change is seen in the pervasiveness of mobile technology, which means more people are connected to more of the world more of the time. This phenomenon is still lopsided; people in the most developed nations are the most connected. But that is changing. Inexpensive smartphones and expanding internet access are proving to be great equalizers. The "global village" is moving from cliché to reality.

These new connections are being used for more than mindless chit-chat and the exchange of cute cat videos. People are learning more about the world around them, and not in passive ways. Their new communication tools allow them to gather information and to converse at levels that have never before been feasible. They can watch what their own and other governments are doing and participate in debate about those doings. They can also use these tools to disseminate information themselves: emailing, posting, tweeting, as well as talking. A few minutes of video on YouTube can be seen worldwide almost instantly, leaping across borders, defying gatekeepers, and stimulating reaction.

When people learn from YouTube or a regional satellite television channel that a young man has set himself on fire because of hopelessness caused by political oppression, the sympathy and anger generated in response can also be transmitted so quickly and widely that a revolution might be born. When people use online networks to tell each other about the plight of refugees who are flooding across borders, compassionate responses might help alleviate the problem. Or, on the darker side, hateful reaction might spread.

All this matters to diplomats because during past centuries their work had proceeded at a measured pace. Theirs was a closed club – elite, male, and disdainful of anyone outside their circle. No more. The ranks of diplomats have been opened to become more inclusive and egalitarian, and the public's attention to their work has grown exponentially.

This was obvious in 2015 in events surrounding the Joint Comprehensive Plan of Action – the Iran nuclear agreement. I have included quite a bit of information about these negotiations and their aftermath because the public's involvement in the debate about the plan provided good examples of the diplomacy that exists beyond the work of professional diplomats. Taking advantage of the connectivity provided by new media tools, especially social media, advocates and opponents of the nuclear deal conducted a global debate designed to influence implementation of the agreement. An issue that once would have remained exclusively the business of a small cadre of diplomats and other officials moved into the public domain. Doors to the world of diplomacy had been thrown wide open, and this affected how the negotiations were conducted and how the surrounding political debate took shape.

This is diplomacy's present, and it foreshadows a fast-evolving future.

I had valuable help with this book. My principal debt is to my wonderful research assistant, Sohaela Amiri. Brilliant and hardworking, she tracked down essential material and steered me away from my tendency to embrace the obscure. Some friends read parts of the manuscript or discussed ideas with me, and they provided valuable insights: Bob Banks, Donna Bragg, Dina Jadallah, Elizabeth Linder, Melody Mohebi, and Andreas Sandre.

At Polity, my editor, Louise Knight, was a joy to work with. She guided me through the entire publishing process, from numerous revisions of my proposal to the final version of the book. She understands my odd temperament and manages it well. Louise's assistant, Nekane Tanaka Galdos was also most helpful and patient. Paul Sharp and an anonymous reviewer provided valuable suggestions about the draft manuscript.

At the University of Southern California, being surrounded by smart colleagues has been a pleasure. Special thanks to Ernest Wilson, Dean of USC's Annenberg School for Communication and Journalism.

I also want to pay tribute to the diplomats, scholars, journalists and others, past and present, whose work has long nurtured my interest in diplomacy. John Lewis Gaddis, Richard Holbrooke, George Kennan, Margaret MacMillan, James Mann, Harold Nicolson, Joseph Nye, David Rothkopf, William Rugh, Mary Elise Sarotte, John Wheeler-Bennett, Lawrence Wright . . . the list is much longer than this and keeps growing.

Most of all, I honor the diplomats and their professional kin who work in often difficult, and sometimes dangerous, circumstances, not only for their own countries, but also to improve the lives of the people amidst whom they serve. They continue to shape the future of diplomacy.

# Introduction

For centuries, diplomacy was the domain of an insular elite. The protagonists worked quietly, often secretly, until ready to unveil their accomplishments or lack thereof. Diplomats were comfortable in this closed environment, speaking just to one another and paying little heed to those publics whose future might be shaped by their work. British diplomat Harold Nicolson, in his 1939 book *Diplomacy*, wrote, "In the days of the old diplomacy it would have been regarded as an act of unthinkable vulgarity to appeal to the common people upon any issue of international policy." He lamented "the invention of the wireless," which gave "a vast impetus to propaganda as a method of policy" and allowed manipulators such as Adolf Hitler to wield "a formidable weapon of popular excitation" that could obstruct or even supersede the work of diplomats.[1]

Today Nicolson's "unthinkable vulgarity" has become integral to diplomacy, and it would be an act of unthinkable stupidity to disregard the "common people" (now more felicitously referred to as "the public") when conducting international relations. The "wireless" of Nicolson's time has evolved into devices that individuals carry in their pockets and consult almost constantly to peruse a vast array of venues ranging from satellite television channels to social media properties such as Twitter and Facebook. For a member of the public to intrude into the diplomatic process may require only a tap on an app.

In this new information era, people gather information from diverse sources, disseminate their own views, and participate in nonstop virtual conversation. The governmental gatekeepers who controlled access to information and shaped much of its content have been nudged aside by the individual seeking out and disseminating "news" as she or he defines it.

Hunger for information has political ramifications, as does the ability of "citizen journalists" with their own agendas to reach large audiences in real time. Diplomats feel the reverberations from this process, and although diplomacy may have been an elitist enterprise for many centuries, it has now, for good or ill, been opened up in the sense that people (at least in democratic societies) can know more about diplomatic activity and can make their voices heard. This is largely the result of media-based empowerment of the public. Diplomats know that speculation as well as solid information about their work will appear quickly and widely. Nothing can be done about that, and so the art of the rapid response has become part of the diplomatic repertoire.

The "popular excitation" that concerned Nicolson can now happen in minutes, as a YouTube video ricochets through online networks and leaps across political boundaries. Diplomats often find themselves compelled to move at a similar pace, responding to the crisis of the moment with little or no time to corroborate information or to reflect on consequences of rapid action. Traditionalists who believe that fast diplomacy is almost always bad diplomacy face a disconcerting reality. They must adapt to a strange and inhospitable new world in which the interests of diverse publics must be addressed quickly, and deciding what to *say* may therefore take precedence over deciding what to *do*.

A central premise of this book is that the future of diplomacy is inextricably tied to the future of media. Much more than speed is involved. The popularization of personal media tools – primarily the mobile phone and including tablets, laptops, and similar devices – empowers individuals in unprecedented ways. People no longer need to rely on traditional news providers, which can be influenced if not controlled by governments. Instead, all those with access to the internet can independently find information about the topics that most interest them on social media venues such as Twitter or through specialized online news services, many existing solely to advance partisan viewpoints. Even more important, members of the public can supplant the traditional relationship between news media and audience by disseminating information through their own networks. In this new media world, everyone can be a journalist of sorts.

The pathways for information extend into the distance. Consider the retweeted tweet. It doesn't go just from A to B and B to C. If B and C retweet it and members of their networks also retweet, its audience can grow exponentially in moments. It may reach thousands of people, few of whom had any connection to the original sender. The information keeps moving, finding its audience and then being pushed ahead to a yet larger audience.

People rely on this process, which is why 500 million tweets are sent every day and 300 hours of video are uploaded to YouTube every minute. This profoundly changes the relationship between the public and institutions such as the BBC, *New York Times*, Reuters, and even relative newcomers such as Al Jazeera and China Central Television (CCTV). These "legacy" news organizations are far less necessary than they once were in maintaining the flow of information.

The new media tools that are changing journalism also reduce the insularity of diplomacy. People expect a river of information, not a trickle, and they expect governments and other societal institutions to contribute to that flow. This requires new levels of transparency in government, including on the part of those who conduct diplomacy, and a commitment by governments to reach out to their own and other publics.

This is another facet of diplomatic practice addressed in this book: "public diplomacy," which in a nutshell means that governments not only must speak to other governments, but also must address global publics – a collective worldwide public or citizens of individual or clusters of countries. Those publics can be accessed through tools such as satellite television and social media. Further, people around the world can talk back to those who wield power and dispense information, and they expect to be listened to. Public diplomacy is no longer just a "nice" thing to do; it has become an essential part of statecraft.

This does not mean that the long slog through the esoteric and sometimes disputatious aspects of negotiation and other diplomatic tasks must always be undertaken in public view. If that were the case, posturing would overwhelm substance even more often than it already does. Rather, the new diplomacy must include a commitment to provide the public with as much information as possible as soon as possible. This is a practical necessity because the information environment has become so porous that doing diplomacy "privately" is decreasingly feasible, as Wikileaks and Edward Snowden's revelations illustrate. Not all diplomacy can be conducted openly, sensitive negotiations may shrivel in sunlight. But there should be a predisposition toward transparency.

Providing information is not a selfless act. Governments use public diplomacy to advance their interests. They do not merely inform; they shape information for their purposes. That said, there are limits to the elasticity of truth, and sometimes the line between truthful "public diplomacy" and misleading "propaganda" becomes blurred. Diplomacy does not exist in an ethical vacuum, and so those who direct public diplomacy must respect the boundaries of honesty. Failure to do so is not only morally irresponsible but also, in an information-rich environment, is likely to be discovered and produce negative results.

In addition to the trend toward democratizing diplomacy that is facilitated by personal media devices, diplomats today must cope with the unprecedented speed at which information-driven events move. A fast-spreading rumor can cause a bloody crisis. A world leader may be compelled to decide whether to take time to respond thoughtfully or act immediately. Ideally, the two could both happen, but to expect that in every case is wishful thinking.

This acceleration has gone on steadily, with new technologies setting the pace: in the nineteenth century, the telegraph and telephone; in the twentieth century, radio and television; in the twenty-first century, social media. It is neither wise nor accurate to scoff at new venues such as YouTube and Facebook as merely homes for soap operas and cat videos. They can suddenly and forcefully intrude into the diplomat's world. If a mosque in Islamabad is blown up and social media chatter says US military personnel were seen nearby, diplomats cannot play for time by saying, "Show us proof." Regardless of whether the allegation is true or not, and regardless of the venue in which it is presented, it may sweep through the public like a forest fire, destroying rationality and igniting passions. Mobs will form in Islamabad and in far-away places, endangering everyone caught in the red-hot updraft.

How can this be dealt with? Only a few decades ago, most angry protests would build slowly enough that governments could craft a response to address the problem before it got out of hand. Today, that cushion of time has become an illusion. The timetable is now based on minutes, not hours or days.

This means that the modern diplomat's training and professional duties must include media skills that extend beyond offering platitudes in front of a television camera and using social media for innocuous, self-serving messaging. "No comment" or "Let me get back to you" may not be tolerated by an audience accustomed only to "NOW."

The new information environment is not only large, it is intellectually competitive. Diplomats' media tactics must conform to public expectations about receiving information, and that information must be able to withstand challenges that come quickly and from many sources. Information disseminated through social media must be part of a larger strategy that advances the home country's interests, and it must be created and dispensed in systematic fashion. Social media use requires a redesign of diplomatic structure to include determination of who should be the social media "spokespersons" for the ministry or embassy, and how the material should be vetted. Several years ago, officials in the US State Department reportedly suggested a rule that all tweets must undergo a two-day approval process before being sent. Two days in the social media world is an eternity. After much derisive laughter, the plan died, but this case underscores how the realities of new media and public expectations clash with traditional diplomatic culture.

In many past cases, "Let's see how things develop" was a wise response to events and was feasible because information moved relatively slowly to policymakers and even more slowly to the public. When President John F. Kennedy received the first, incomplete information about construction of what was to become the Berlin Wall, he determined that no American lives were in danger and there was no need for an immediate, provocative response. So, he said nothing publicly and went sailing. Several days passed before news coverage fully caught up with the story, and there were no alternative media sources that could speed the process. Kennedy had time to gather facts, weigh policy alternatives, and proceed deliberately.

Today, however, the public may become aware of events at the same time or even before policymakers learn what is happening. With media voices of all kinds yapping about the need to "do something," it can be tempting to set aside wise caution in favor of dramatic expediency. The results may range from unfortunate to disastrous.

The "Arab spring" uprisings of 2011 exemplify the high-speed environment in which diplomats work today. In countries such as Egypt, information of varying accuracy was flowing at great volume and great speed. Internal messaging, primarily using social media, helped the anti-government movement retain cohesion, while external audiences in the region and beyond could keep track of events in real time thanks to Arab satellite television channels as well as Facebook, YouTube, and the like. Governments found that these media were outpacing their own diplomatic and other sources. At the White House, most televisions were tuned to Al Jazeera English as a fast and relatively reliable means of keeping abreast of developments in the Arab states. Traditionally, the US embassy in Cairo would have been the main source of updates about events, but embassy personnel cannot keep pace with thousands of individuals gathering and disseminating information. Even intelligence agencies cannot match the speed of Twitter.

The "Arab spring" case illustrates how new media have replaced the diplomatic pouch and most traditional news providers as the way some information is delivered to governments. This necessitates increasingly sophisticated monitoring of media sites. Keeping track of dozens or even hundreds of satellite television channels' content is feasible, but mining the veins of social media is far more challenging because of the size of the task and the difficulty of judging veracity.

Public diplomacy has been developed in different ways by different countries, and sometimes differently by diplomats from the same country. A recent Mexican ambassador to the United States was the first foreign diplomat in Washington to use Twitter as an official tool, and he did so frequently, in Spanish and English, reaching out to the Mexican diaspora in the United States as well as audiences in Mexico and the rest of Latin America and the world. His successor, on the other hand, did not see fit to use Twitter at all.

China has invested heavily in public diplomacy, relying on its CCTV broadcasts in numerous languages, its Confucius Institute cultural centers, its aid programs in Africa and elsewhere, and other initiatives. Chinese diplomats rely less on social media than do their counterparts from other nations, perhaps because the Chinese government prefers control rather than spontaneity in its diplomacy. This might be unrealistic. Despite concerted efforts to control online access and content, Chinese officialdom may soon realize that they are trying to hold back the tide.

These examples and others make clear that the newest kind of diplomacy is not uniform and is still evolving. Throughout this book, cases illustrate this. Any nation that fails to take seriously the transformative power of new media will be limiting its diplomatic effectiveness. Today's publics expect a degree of participatory diplomacy, meaning that the old model of directing messages *at* an audience is being replaced by communicating *with* the audience. People who grow accustomed in their personal lives to the back-and-forth of social media are likely to expect governments to likewise engage with their constituents, which in the era of globalization includes diverse and far-flung groups.

Moving farther beyond their traditionally cloistered practice, diplomats have increasingly become involved in shaping public opinion. Again, media tools are at the heart of this. An example is the Israel–Gaza conflict of 2014. In addition to the purely military aspects of this, both sides engaged in a diplomatic battle as they tried to shape news organizations' coverage and also deliver their versions of the aggressor–victim debate directly to global publics through social media.

The Palestinians know that in conventional battlefield terms, the Israelis will almost always prevail, but media messaging can be a political equalizer of sorts. This is not a matter of simply tweeting occasionally. For diplomacy at this level to be successful requires creative and consistent use of numerous social media forums, such as using YouTube to disseminate video that major news organizations may consider too graphic, one-sided, or unverifiable.

Public diplomacy is important because public opinion matters. Especially in democracies, those who make and implement foreign policy ignore their own and global publics at their peril. Secret backroom deals, such as victors carving up their territorial prizes of war, are unlikely to remain secret for long; too many people with access to inside information are eager to talk about it, and social media offer appealing ways to do so. Nevertheless, lips sometimes remain sealed (and fingers remain off the mobile phone keyboard). The recent US–Cuba negotiations were kept secret, which was a diplomatic necessity, given how politically charged the issue was. Crafty secrecy is still possible and, at times, still essential.

In the future of diplomacy, public diplomacy will be central, and diplomats of nations that aspire to being viewed as major players in world affairs will need to work with publics that their professional predecessors could ignore.

Although diplomacy, at least since the seventeenth century, has primarily concerned itself with relationships among states, non-state actors have achieved new prominence on the global stage. Some are disruptive, others are constructive, in their effects on world affairs. This is another central element of this book.

As of this writing, in mid-2015, the Middle East serves as a showcase for the disruptive power that non-state actors can wield.

An army of mostly Sunni militants seized sizable portions of Iraq and Syria and proclaimed itself the Islamic State – IS, also known as ISIS, ISIL, and Daesh. No government recognizes IS as a state, but numerous governments have recognized its grim prowess and attacked it. IS aspires to some kind of statehood, and if it survives, this will pose challenges to the global diplomatic community.

IS is a descendant of a branch of Al Qaeda, another non-state entity, which had the wherewithal to attack the United States. Using online media venues, IS achieved global reach for its propaganda and recruiting efforts. Such non-states cannot be ignored, but how are they to be dealt with – if at all – diplomatically?

There are also benign non-state actors, non-governmental organizations such as Doctors Without Borders, which have enhanced their influence by skillfully using the same media tools that states employ – their own kind of public diplomacy. They can pull public attention to humanitarian emergencies and do this so compellingly that governments must include them in diplomatic calculations. The Ebola crisis of 2014 in parts of West Africa illustrated how non-state actors can help shape the global issues agenda and engage with governments to achieve their policy goals.

We can add to the mix the international organizations such as the United Nations, the World Bank, and numerous others that have been established since the Second World War. The breadth of diplomacy keeps expanding, and its practices adapt accordingly.

Diplomatic responsibilities have grown and will continue to do so, but they are not limitless. Partisan politics and diplomacy rarely work well together, and yet the diminished insularity of diplomats opens their work to greater political interference. This can lead to the assignment of inappropriate tasks to diplomats and confusion about who is in charge of diplomacy. In the United States, for example, the White House and the State Department share diplomatic duties with other parts of the executive branch ranging from the Department of Defense to the Department of Agriculture. The legislative branch maintains oversight and controls budgets, and is not shy about interjecting itself into diplomatic matters.

In a global society, it is logical that domestic and international responsibilities will mingle, but it may be that diplomacy is becoming so bureaucratized and politicized that its effectiveness will diminish. Diplomacy's future will depend in part on its role being better defined and its operations being made more efficient.

With all these matters taken into consideration, it is clear that the future of diplomacy will not be merely a technology-enhanced continuation of traditional roles. The diplomat's fundamental mission is changing. Diplomats were once primarily negotiators and providers of information to their governments. They talked to one another, not to the public. They still negotiate and embassies still gather information, but in addition they are directly accountable to the public. Their direct constituencies have expanded. When an American secretary of state emerges from a negotiating session with China, Iran, Russia, or any other country, she or he speaks to news correspondents and instantly social media pick up on those comments and are filled with speculation about what is "really" happening. The Secretary then tweets her or his own message. As of mid-2015, US Secretary of State John Kerry had 478,000 followers on Twitter, and assuming a reasonable number of retweets, his viewpoint could reach millions almost instantly. His diplomatic counterparts might act similarly, and cyberspace becomes thick with information about the negotiations. Some of it is accurate.

Given their increased visibility and expanded public responsibilities, top-level diplomats, such as the US Secretary of State, are now chosen for their political acumen as much as for their foreign policy expertise. In part this is because an experienced politician knows how to negotiate deals, but also because the opening up of the diplomatic process creates many more media-related demands. In the United States, shrewd political figures such as James Baker, Colin Powell, and Hillary Rodham Clinton have served as Secretary of State and exemplified the high-octane mix of diplomatic and political talents. They are media savvy as well as being attuned to traditional diplomatic duties.

Not all diplomats will be in senior roles or have "rock star" credentials, so their training must prepare them to undertake tasks such as using media tools to gradually engage with foreign publics. Some embassies now include video production teams on their staffs so they can provide social media content with the frequency and quality that global constituencies – especially younger people – have come to expect. This facet of the media environment is highly competitive, and some diplomats may resent what they see as their job becoming that of a "television programmer." Regardless of this reluctance, the diplomat's work in the future will, to some extent, be tied to media proficiency.

Once the expanding role of the individual diplomat is understood and accepted, making the transformation in training and in practice should not be difficult. But reshaping diplomacy as an endeavor of nations may be more challenging. Even "hermit kingdoms" such as North Korea have come to recognize that power does not reside solely in missiles, and influence is not exercised only secretly. Countries within the mainstream of international relations must become more sophisticated in their recognition that the "democratization" many of them have endorsed is arriving in unanticipated ways.

Diplomacy that operates as a closed club is not yet obsolete, but that approach is increasingly seen as archaic and ineffective. The mechanisms of foreign policy must conform to the expectations of an energized public. The future of diplomacy will be shaped by new media, new publics, and new manifestations of political power.

# 1

# Open Diplomacy

To refine one of this book's central themes, it is worth keeping in mind that while diplomacy is increasingly shaped by tools such as social media, there are limits to this. It is important not to allow fascination with media gadgetry to produce a distorted view of how diplomacy works. The effectiveness of any tool depends on how it is used.

First, let's be wary about the term "digital diplomacy." Although it has become highly fashionable, the term is misleading in that it may be taken as ascribing greater significance to technology than is deserved. Diplomacy is at its heart a process dependent on policy and people. Technology – digital or otherwise – provides an array of tools to make that process more efficient. But technology is soulless, and as such its value in diplomacy, while important, has limits.

That said, new technologies are profoundly changing societies and cultures around the world, affecting everything from sports to medicine, and certainly including diplomacy. As for media, a case can be made that the internet is the most transformative phenomenon since the arrival of the movable-type printing press in the fifteenth century. Just as Johannes Gutenberg's invention allowed dissemination of ideas to ever-growing audiences, today's internet-based communication fosters an even more widespread and participatory expansion of knowledge.

This is the environment in which the future of diplomacy is taking shape. As the newest media tools come into play, reliance on technology becomes more problematic. Granted, some who rely on digital tools see them as just that – tools. But it is best to embrace only cautiously anything that seems a panacea for reaching global publics. The availability of a service like Twitter – such an easy way to communicate – makes its use irresistible, regardless of how suitable it might be in a particular profession or situation. Such is the problem of putting the virtual cart ahead of the not necessarily virtual horse.

Regardless of how diplomats decide to employ these tools, much of the rest of the world is busy using them. Consider some basic statistics (and note the youthfulness of these transformative enterprises):

- Facebook, born in 2004, and so the oldest of the social media giants, had 1.55 billion active monthly users as of September 2015.
- YouTube, created in 2005, also has more than a billion users, and they upload more than 300 hours of video every minute.
- Twitter, which came onto the scene in 2006, sees 500 million tweets every day, 80 percent of which come from mobile devices. (As of March 2015, the Twitter user with the most fol-lowers was singer Katy Perry, with 67 million. She was closely

followed by another singer, Justin Bieber, with 61 million, and President Barack Obama, who had 56 million followers.)

- Instagram began in 2010, hosting 70 million photos each day and sharing a total of more than 30 billion photographs.
- Sina Weibo, a Chinese service that combines attributes of Facebook and Twitter, was created in 2009, has 600 million users, 70 percent of whom access it through their mobile devices. (Sina Weibo's most popular user as of early 2015 was actor Chen Kun, who had 73 million followers.)

So what does all this mean? Are "friends" on Facebook really friends? Only if an exceptionally broad definition of "friendship" holds sway. Are Chen Kun and Katy Perry the two most popular people in the world? Doubtful, but what does "popular" mean today?

What about Instagram and its kin? Have tens of millions of people become exhibitionists and voyeurs, eager to post and peruse photographs of themselves and others? Yes, but most of them probably do not think of themselves that way. They like to say they are "sharing."

Regardless of motives and judgments, numbers at these levels are evidence of more than just a surge of popular interest in entertainers and visual gossip. People want to receive and produce "information," defined broadly, and so the social media industry continues to expand. Between when this is written and when it is published, more social media providers will appear. Some will not have the financial stamina to survive for long; some promising ones might be swallowed, in exchange for considerable riches, by established companies; and a few will endure, at least for a while, and perhaps find a viable user base.

Social media have been dismissed by some as just the latest fad of Americans and other Western elites. But statistics about Facebook illustrate geographic as well as numerical growth. In the period from the first quarter of 2013 through the first quarter of 2015, daily active Facebook users worldwide increased from 665 million to 936 million. Of that increase, users in the United States and Canada went from 139 million to 161 million, a growth of 16 percent. Meanwhile, Facebook usage in the rest of the world grew from 526 million to 775 million daily users, a 47 percent increase. The overall distribution of the 936 million daily users is 161 million in the United States and Canada, 225 million in Europe, 270 million in the Asia-Pacific region, and 280 million in the rest of the world.[1] Twitter also reports substantial international growth. The service supports 33 languages and 77 percent of its accounts are outside the United States.[2]

A significant imbalance clearly remains, but looking ahead it is safe to say that rapid expansion of internet and social media use will continue. Prices of "computers" – especially the mobile versions – continue to drop. As of 2015, a US$40 smartphone was entering the marketplace, and ingenious ways were being devised to bring the internet to previously isolated regions. Google has been working on Project Loon, a way to deliver wireless service by using a high-altitude (about 20 miles up) balloon network. Tests of Loon in 2013 in New Zealand were successful.[3]

With much evidence pointing to continued expansion of the social media user base, many in the foreign policy establishment look at the numbers and jump into this new world. By summer 2014, the US State Department hosted 230 Facebook pages, 80 Twitter accounts, 55 YouTube channels, and 40 Flickr accounts.[4] Also in mid-2014, the United Nations' main Twitter profile had almost 3 million followers and its Facebook page had more than 1.1 million friends. Overall, the UN managed 18 Facebook pages, 25 Twitter profiles, two Tumblr blogs, two LinkedIn pages (including that of the Secretary-General), and also had accounts on YouTube, Pinterest, Google+, Flickr, Instagram, and Weibo.[5]

With this kind of activity, a great temptation exists to celebrate a marriage between diplomacy and social media. But the number and diversity of digital venues being used does not necessarily have anything to do with *diplomacy*. Volume is nice, but content is what really matters.

This is nothing new. "Revolutionary" communication tools have popped up regularly for centuries. For our purposes, their impact in two areas is worth examining: how they affected the public's knowledge of the world around them, and how diplomats and those responsible for designing foreign policy responded to that expansion of knowledge.

## Some history: communication technology evolves

Depending on how one defines "communication technology," the timeline can begin many thousands of years ago with the instruments used to paint animals on cave walls and chisel symbols onto stone tablets. For our purposes, we will leap into relatively modern times – the nineteenth century – and use the arrival of the telegraph as the starting point for examining intersections between media and diplomacy. The future is built upon the past.

After many experiments, electric telegraphy came of age in 1837, and in 1866 the first successful trans-Atlantic cable was completed. This soon changed the nature of diplomacy. No longer did news between North America and Europe need to travel on ships, which meant that no longer did wars continue long after peace terms had been agreed upon, as had happened in the War of 1812 between Britain and the United States when news of the Treaty of Ghent took a month to reach combatants.

But was the impact of the telegraph entirely positive? In his study of the telegraph's effects on diplomacy, David Paul Nickles observes that "delays in diplomacy produced by ship-carried dispatches provided time for tempers to cool and peacemakers to go about their work." Nickles cites the 1861 *Trent* affair, during the American Civil War, when a Union warship stopped and boarded the British mail steamer *Trent*, on which were two Confederate diplomats en route to England. The Union sailors seized the two Confederates and took them to the US mainland as prisoners while the *Trent* went on its way. When news of the event reached London, the prime minister, Lord Palmerston, and others immediately began talking about war against the Union government of the United States. Nickles writes: "The *Trent* affair provides an instance when the use of the telegraph in diplomacy, by eliminating periods of delay, would have created more problems than it solved. During intervals of waiting, initial reactions could be questioned, participants could compose themselves, and plans could be reconsidered, all with generally beneficial results." The British ambassador to the United States, Lord Lyons, had moved cautiously during the controversy and offered a valuable diplomatic axiom, "Never do anything today that can be put off until tomorrow."[6]

The telephone soon superseded the telegraph. It may be considered the first social media device in that it enhanced the ability of individuals to communicate with one another, regardless of physical proximity, and with a personal directness that the telegraph did not permit.

The telephone's importance in a political context is that it facilitates communication about ideas and events. Everyday discussion expanded; family and friends, even those at considerable distance, could become members of networks, sharing information and then passing it along. Almost all phone calls were one-to-one, and so those networks remained linear and were nothing like what we see today with Twitter and such. But the methodical, person-to-person transmission of information changed the ways people saw themselves and the world. As the phone call pushed aside the letter, a broader kind of literacy developed. The spoken word was no longer just for face-to-face communication. It reached across the street and eventually across the planet.

Diplomats found their work altered by the telephone in several ways. First, the immediacy of telephonic connection tightened the linkage between diplomats in the field and their bosses, and so reduced operational autonomy. More significantly – although harder to grasp and measure – discourse about foreign policy expanded among individuals, at least in democracies. More people could learn about an international event through the news media and then refine and share their opinions during telephone conversations, creating a ripple effect that sometimes – depending on the salience of the issue – would build enough momentum to capture policymakers' attention. Again, this foreshadowed today's social media network phenomena.

Even in less stressful circumstances, the telephone changed diplomats' work. Lessened reliance on the written word in favor of the more transient qualities of speech was viewed warily by those concerned that the casualness of conversation could distort the nuanced communication of diplomacy. Even given its ubiquity, the telephone allows "mass communication" in only a micro sense – individual to individual. This progression can continue indefinitely, but the audience, small or large, is reached piecemeal.

The arrival of radio had far different ramifications. Radio technology evolved quickly during the first two decades of the twentieth century, and by the 1920s commercial radio broadcasts were underway in the United States, United Kingdom, and elsewhere. Audiences grew quickly. In 1921, 60,000 American homes had radios and 30 radio stations were on the air. By 1940, radios were to be found in 29 million US homes (out of a total 35 million American households), tuned in to 814 stations.[7]

The radio became an essential part of many families' lives mainly because it delivered hour upon hour of entertainment: music, sports, comedy, drama. But it was as a provider of news that it most shaped people's perceptions of the world around them and so affected the work of diplomats.

Consider how the war in Europe in 1940 was depicted in American homes and why this mattered. Nazi Germany's military had rolled through much of Western Europe and only Britain remained an obstacle in its path. But Britain was in desperate straits, short on munitions and money, and enduring savage *Luftwaffe* bombing raids. Aid from the United States was desperately needed, but many Americans had Europe fatigue. Barely 20 years had passed since American troops had been sent to fight in the Great War, and few in the United States were interested in helping clean up another European mess. Isolationism offered a cocoon that seemed far preferable to involvement.

Radio helped pierce that cocoon. American radio reporters – most famously Edward R. Murrow of CBS – provided dramatic on-site accounts about Britain under siege. Gradually, these reports, plus the shrewd political leadership of President Franklin D. Roosevelt, weaned Americans from isolationism and allowed a lifeline of aid to be established across the Atlantic.

Reporting such as Murrow's real-time accounts of the London blitz was a principal factor in this shift. In a 1941 tribute to Murrow, American literary figure Archibald MacLeish said: "You destroyed in the minds of many men and women in this country the superstition that what is done beyond three thousand miles of water is not really done at all . . .. You burned the city of London in our houses and we felt the flames that burned it. You laid the dead of London at our doors and we knew the dead were our dead."[8] Diplomats have learned that such "living-room war" can have substantial effect on the publics to which policymakers are accountable.

By the mid-1950s, radio faced increasing competition from a still newer technology: television. In terms of influencing how global publics saw the world, television's images transcended even the word pictures of radio masters such as Murrow. For diplomats, this was another shift in the balance of influence. With radio, people could hear for themselves what was happening, as in London during the blitz, but with television they could *see* what was happening – everything from baseball to battlefields. If what they saw conflicted with what they had been told by official sources, they were likely – especially over time – to trust their own eyes.

Within the foreign affairs community, diplomats' role as interpreters of world events was altered. Their reports from the field might clash with depictions foreign ministry officials saw on the television screen. In their relationships with officials and publics of other countries, diplomats increasingly had to contend with, "But I saw on television . . ." Diplomats had always faced information competition, but television was one more step in making that competition more contentious.

This gets to the context in which diplomats must work. The insularity of their professional environment has diminished. Television coverage of conflicts and humanitarian emergencies gave rise to a "CNN effect," in which graphic television images were presumed to influence public opinion to the extent that diplomatic strategies had to be adjusted to conform to the world as depicted on the TV screen.

Diplomats generally consider this a harmful distraction. Writing in his diary about the US intervention in Somalia in 1993, retired American diplomat George F. Kennan considered why Congress and the public so readily acceded to the military/humanitarian commitment: "There can be no question that the reason for this acceptance lies primarily with the exposure of the Somalia situation by the American media; above all, television. The reaction would have been unthinkable without this exposure. The reaction was an emotional one, occasioned by the sight of the suffering of the starving people in question." Kennan added that "if American policy from here on out, particularly policy involving the use of our armed forces abroad, is to be controlled by popular emotional impulses, and especially ones provoked by the commercial television industry, then there is no place not only for myself, but for the responsible deliberative organs of our government."[9]

Kennan's dire appraisal of television's influence was not solely the opinion of someone whose diplomatic career had been largely undisturbed by unwanted intrusions from the mass media.

His outlook was shared by some representatives of those same media. *New York Times* television critic Walter Goodman had commented two years before the Somalia intervention, on the occasion of Western countries providing military protection for Iraqi Kurds, that "a picture that arouses sympathy does not necessarily enhance understanding," and he asked, "Should American policy be driven by scenes that happen to be accessible to cameras and make the most impact on the screen?"[10]

Perhaps, in a democracy, policy *should* be affected by scenes that "make the most impact on the screen." If the public wants its country to intervene somewhere, maybe diplomatic strategy should conform to that desire. On the other hand, news coverage, particularly on television, may present a deceptively simplistic view of a complex issue, "touching the heart without reaching the brain."[11]

This takes us into questions about the extent to which foreign policymaking should retain at least some of its elitist traits. Mass media content can generate momentum toward a more egalitarian approach that caters to the public opinion of the moment. How informed is that opinion? This is a debate that Kennan's professional descendants will contend with more and more in our increasingly media-rich environment.

Kennan wrote about Somalia at the time television was taking another technological step forward: live coverage of breaking news. This reached its first major milestone in November 1963 during the aftermath of President John F. Kennedy's assassination. The gravitational pull of a household's television set was in evidence when the funeral procession began: 93 percent of American televisions were tuned in to the coverage. Globally, the Telstar satellite, which had carried its first broadcasts in 1962, provided coverage of the Kennedy funeral to 23 countries around the world.[12]

This television coverage also served an important political function. ABC News president Elmer Lower later wrote: "Television held this nation together for four days, keeping people informed by a steady flow of news, and showing them vividly that President Johnson had taken command of the situation and that the transfer of power had taken place smoothly . . . The steady flow of news gave a sense of confidence."[13]

For diplomats, lessons were to be learned from this intensive coverage. First, real-time news coverage – assuming it is accurate – can be crucial in preventing the spread of unfounded rumors and tamping down public rage or panic. Second, television can be a national, or even worldwide, unifier, as people receive information and experience emotions simultaneously. The notion of a "global village" becomes real.

That village, however, comprises many neighborhoods that may have little in common. Their residents may look at news differently, depending on who is delivering it and what political and cultural characteristics are reflected in the coverage of people and events. The success of Al Jazeera is a good example of this.

For many years, Arabs had to rely on Western news providers such as the BBC and CNN for information about the world at large and even about their own slice of that world. Arab television news was largely state-run, dull, and heavily censored. Al Jazeera was born in 1996, and quickly distinguished itself through its lively programming and high production values. By the time of the Second Intifada in 2000, it was able to deliver news about Arabs *as seen through Arab eyes*. During the next decade, while war raged in Iraq, Arabs looked to Al Jazeera (and other channels such as Al

Arabiya and Al Manar) to provide news that fit comfortably within their worldview. When conflicts exploded between Palestinians and Israelis, there was no question in Arab minds about which side *their* television newscasters were on. Western hegemony in news dissemination was eroding, and new voices were contributing to political restlessness and change.

Playing to political sentiment in the Middle East is not limited to Arab channels. RT (formerly known as Russia Today) has an Arabic-language channel that has become popular in the Arab world. This is not because of any great love for Russia, but because the channel's content is consistently anti-American, which sits well with many Arabs.

Diplomats found that these new broadcasters made even more volatile an already unstable region. Matters that once might have been negotiated quietly were now being presented to the Arab public in ways that put new political pressure on their governments, and diplomats had to adapt to this edgier political context.

Beyond the Middle East, regional satellite television markets have become heavily populated by government-operated news channels that deliver their versions of events in numerous languages. China's CCTV, for example, has overseas channels broadcasting in English, Spanish, French, Arabic, and Russian (with Portuguese soon to come), and in Mandarin to reach members of the Chinese diaspora who prefer their traditional language.

These channels produce a cacophony of competing voices that diplomats must deal with in a number of ways. None of this is new. Nations have long used broadcasting to deploy truth and propaganda against one another, some more skillfully than others. What *is* new, however, is the amount of information and the speed at which it moves. This requires new levels of diplomatic agility.

## The internet and smartphones arrive

The arrival of the mobile telephone was yet another quantum leap forward. It untethered users from the limitations of landlines. Communication takes place when the consumer wants it. For many people, the mobile phone has become an appendage, and being without it is traumatic. Setting it aside even briefly is like dropping off your child at daycare for the first time.

The mobile phone's use for only voice and text has been superseded by the smartphone, which provides connection to the internet. Today, there are 7 billion humans on the planet and 6 billion mobile phones, of which 2 billion are smartphones. By 2020, smartphones are expected to surpass 4 billion in number, and they will no longer be limited primarily to those who can pay upwards of US$500 for expensive versions such as an Apple iPhone. As prices continue to fall, smartphone use will cross lines of geography and class.

Sociologists have decades' worth of studies ahead of them as they consider how this connectivity affects relationships among individuals, communities, and institutions. For diplomats, the most important issues, at least for now, are speed and directness of contact, and the opening to the public of vast reservoirs of information that can be tapped via the internet.

Some basic principles to keep in mind regarding the impact of the internet on diplomacy are these:

- Particularly with the increasing availability of smartphones and online connectivity, the internet is approaching truly global reach, more so than any other medium.
- The amount of information available through internet-based

media is so vast, it can be exceptionally difficult to monitor, much less control, and analyzing it requires big-data tools.

- Online material moves instantaneously, both directly and through networks. Reacting with similar quickness is not always necessary or wise.

- The public is no longer passive; it expects to participate. People do not just read a newspaper or watch a television program and keep their reactions to themselves. Instead, they pass along information within their networks (such as their Facebook friends), often adding their own commentary. They may also respond directly to the sources of the information, and they expect those sources to answer in turn. As anyone who has spent hours replying to emails knows, this process requires redefining duties and work habits. Diplomats are not exempt from this.

From such fundamental premises new facets of diplomatic practice must be designed. Consider, for instance, that some of the information reaching people so quickly is, for whatever reason, not accurate. Often this is just a matter of sloppiness – a failure to meet basic standards of verification and corroboration. But sometimes spreading bad information is purposeful, and it may inspire an angry – even bloody – response. Such was the case in 2012 of *Innocence of Muslims*.

You would think that if a trailer for a film existed, that the film would as well. But for *Innocence of Muslims*, only a ten-minute trailer ever emerged, and it was a sophomoric, barely coherent slander against Islam. It portrayed the Prophet Mohammed as a sex-fiend and bloodthirsty thug. Any Muslim would certainly be offended, as would many non-Muslims, and some might become so angry that they would seek an outlet for their fury.

It was just a snippet of film and it appeared only once in a movie theater – in Hollywood, California before an audience of about ten persons. But because of the internet, it was visible to the world. The original English-language version was soon dubbed in Arabic and could be watched on YouTube. Under American law, it was hateful but not illegal, so YouTube did not pull it down.

Meanwhile, also on the internet, word of the "American film's" content spread by email and social media. Many who did not actually see the material were nonetheless angered by its mere existence, and some – in Egypt, for instance – took to the streets and targeted the US embassy to vent their anger. Violent protests also erupted in Yemen, India, Tunisia, and at US diplomatic outposts elsewhere. Tens of thousands of demonstrators participated, and there were numerous casualties. Information spread by word of mouth was nothing new; what had changed with "word of internet" was speed and reach.

Worth keeping in mind is that less than a decade before, YouTube did not exist and so the world would have been spared *Innocence of Muslims*. But YouTube is so easily accessible and its content so easily shared that the inflammatory video could be watched by millions. As valuable and constructive as the internet can be, it can also resemble an open sewer, with similarly noxious effect.

In such fast-moving cases, those who must respond may find themselves needing to react before they possess sufficient facts. Henry Kissinger observed:

Policymakers are expected to have formulated a position within several hours and to interject it into the course of events – where its effects will be broadcast globally by the same instantaneous networks. The temptation to cater to the demands of the digitally reflected multitude may override the judgment required to chart a complex course in harmony with long-term purposes. The distinction between information, knowledge, and wisdom is weakened.[14]

Eventually, *Innocence of Muslims* receded into the obscurity it deserved, but the chaos it precipitated stands as a warning about the savagery of speed. Diplomats cannot stop the movement of information, so they now must develop contingency plans that will allow them to react to worst-case scenarios that are certain to arise from time to time in the new media environment. As with speech generally, the best way to respond to information that you don't like is with more information. In an instance such as the *Innocence of Muslims* case, diplomats trying to offset public anger should have previously identified Muslim clerics on whom they could call to promptly deliver counter-messaging. This is the kind of tactic that, although not certain to be successful, can be employed while broader strategy is devised.

## Security and privacy

For the diplomat who has been blindsided by an unforeseen crisis, contingency planning might seem the highest priority. But changes in security and privacy that are related to new media technologies can be difficult to anticipate. Say "Wikileaks" and watch a diplomat twitch.

As the computer came to dominate communication, the conventional wisdom was this: secure computer means secure document. The problem: few people really understood what "secure" meant.

One who did was Australian activist Julian Assange, who established Wikileaks in 2006. Basically, Wikileaks acts as an intermediary for whistleblowers, receiving documents, videos, and other information in which the public might be interested. Wikileaks posts information on its website and distributes material to news organizations for publication. Among Wikileaks' most famous early releases was the gunsight video of a 2007 US helicopter attack in Baghdad that killed several journalists and other civilians.

Wikileaks soon moved into the dissemination of massive amounts of material, and in November 2010 began releasing more than 250,000 classified US State Department cables. They had been stolen by a US government employee who delivered them to Assange. These included field reports from American diplomats about political figures and other topics in the countries where they were serving. Some of these appraisals were less than flattering to their subjects. Wikileaks provided the material to selected newspapers around the world, and the news media served up juicy tidbits, such as information about the United States eavesdropping on United Nations Secretary General Kofi Annan shortly before the US invasion of Iraq in 2003. More recent Wikileaks releases have included guidelines from the Central Intelligence Agency about how its operatives might pass through airport security while using phony identification.

How much real harm Wikileaks has done to US diplomacy is debatable; embarrassment does not necessarily equate to lasting damage. But although some observers noted that the release of the cables showed American diplomats to be quite good writers, it perhaps more significantly demonstrated that the new medium of choice for diplomatic communication – the email – can be tampered with at least as successfully as embassy letters could be steamed open in olden days.

Hacking into government computers will be an ongoing competition, with governments erecting higher walls around their communications, and hackers – governments and private operators – devising new ways to scale those walls. Diplomats will need to recognize that security in the high-tech era can be illusory.

So, too, can *privacy* be an illusion. The computerized tools that foster fast and far-reaching communication are no less susceptible to eavesdropping than is a telephone landline that can be tapped. Spying by the US National Security Agency was revealed by Edward Snowden, a computer expert working for an NSA contractor, who took almost two million documents (mostly American) that he said revealed, among other things, illegal NSA eavesdropping. News media reported, beginning in 2013, that those whose communications were surveilled without notice included American citizens and foreign leaders, such as German Chancellor Angela Merkel. Private citizens' email content was being reviewed, as were their contact lists. Online game players, such as devotees of "World of Warcraft," were being watched, and so were organizations including UNICEF and Brazil's petroleum company, Petrobas. The list goes on.

The legal and ethical issues raised by Snowden's leaks are profound as they relate to the balance between "national security" and the right to privacy, matters that are mostly outside the scope of this book. On a practical level, diplomats were affected by the revelations in several ways. American diplomats had to deal with furious victims of the eavesdropping, such as Merkel, and others in their governments. (Some of these leaders' complaints could be viewed as disingenuous given their own spy services' practices – or at least their aspirations.) Beyond that, at least as debilitating was the evidence that almost nothing can be kept secret, that communications within the foreign affairs community – between diplomats in the field and their ministries, and among diplomats themselves – could be thoroughly surveilled. It had long been supposed that spy agencies might have the capacity to intrude this way, and Snowden's material both proved that this was happening and astonished people with the breadth of computer-enabled surveillance.

In this respect at least, the "new media revolution" has not lived up to its promise of facilitating greater globalized egalitarianism. The powerful find new ways to accumulate and abuse power, and the work of diplomats – and that of many others – can be seriously impeded. Diplomats' future duties must therefore be designed with full recognition of contemporary limits on the privacy of communication.

Regardless of its flaws, this is the environment in which diplomacy must shape its future. The hyper-connected world will lend itself to wider use by the public and will become more densely populated with devices during the coming years. Again, some statistics:

- Four times more data were expected to be generated in 2015 than in 2011.
- By 2018, there will be 21 billion networked devices globally, up from 12 billion in 2013.
- In 2018, people will upload more than 350 million photographs to social media sites each day.

- As for economic impact, in the United States as of 2014, the digital economy had accounted for about 7 percent of GDP and for 37 percent of economic growth since the mid-1990s. Since early in the twenty-first century, about 40 percent of new US jobs have come from new technologies.[15]

So, we are not talking about a mere techie fad. This is a transformational time, and not for diplomats alone.

## The empowered public

In 1994, when nearly a million people were slaughtered in Rwanda without the world taking timely notice, what would have happened if people there had had smartphones, with their cameras and the ability to connect to the internet? How many lives would have been saved if images from the killing grounds had quickly appeared on YouTube and reached governments and news organizations around the globe? If visible to the world, murder on that scale would, one hopes, have elicited a response, perhaps prompt military intervention that might have saved hundreds of thousands of lives.

Technological optimists might contend that the smartphone would have been the tool to pull together the global village, and the Rwandans' fellow villagers would have come to their rescue. But would that have happened? Look around the world today and focus on Syria for a moment. As this is written in mid-2015, the death toll in that war has passed 250,000 and more than two million Syrians are refugees. Murder, rape, enslavement, use of chemical weapons . . . the horror of Syria is overwhelming. And smartphones are there.

Video emerges, as does victims' testimony, and yet most of the rest of the world cannot decide how – or even if – to respond in meaningful ways. Granted, the politics of the situation are complicated, but there is no denying that the world knows, with the help of new communication technologies, more about what is going on in Syria than was the case in many past crises. Knowledge in itself is not determinative.

Those diplomats who want to bring an end to the war desperately need global publics to pressure governments and international organizations to take decisive action. But for whatever reason – perhaps compassion fatigue – this has not happened. One factor contributing to this inaction may be that the new technologies are providing so much information about so many wars and other humanitarian disasters that no single instance, regardless of how horrific it might be, can capture and hold public attention.

Being able to access lots of information has generally been considered to be a good thing. But can it be too much of a good thing? Pete Cashmore, founder of online news provider Mashable, has pointed out that "content is not a scarce resource; attention is a scarce resource," and Charles Firestone of the Aspen Institute has noted that "the ability to get attention is a real asset, as attention is the real scarcity with the overabundance of information."[16]

Diplomats trying to bring about peace in a conflict, to secure aid after a natural disaster, or to otherwise be helpful to people in need, have long understood that getting and retaining attention from policymakers and publics is essential. The "CNN effect" was assumed to be useful in this regard, providing dramatic video images from Somalia, Bosnia, Ethiopia – crises that elicited emergency assistance (of varying effectiveness). But neither the CNN effect a few years ago nor the spread of connectivity today has proved to be a moral panacea.

In circumstances such as these, diplomats may puzzle over how to best put new technologies to work in shaping public opinion and governmental action. The media landscape is so crowded that centers of influence have shrunk to the point at which they have little effect. In 1984, when one American television network, NBC, broadcast a story about famine in Ethiopia, the results were instantaneous and measurable. Within a few days, relief agencies reported a surge of contributions, and the Reagan administration announced it would significantly expand its food aid to Ethiopia. One NBC executive observed: "This [famine] has been going on for a long time, and nobody cared. Now it's on TV and everybody cares."[17]

Diplomats, aid workers, and others who had championed Ethiopian relief could pursue a straightforward media strategy: get a major television network to air dramatic pictures and the public will see them and demand action. But today there is no longer any such thing as a "major network"; the media pie has been sliced into many narrow pieces. Building momentum behind a cause requires an entirely different media strategy, one that relies at least as much on social media venues such as Facebook as it does on traditional media.

Related to this are issues of accuracy and credibility. Governments and a finite number of media entities used to be the principal influencers. Despite news organizations' protestations of independence, a de facto alliance has always existed between governments and many in the news media. Government officials became adept at using instruments such as CNN or the *New York Times* to validate their policy positions. During the run-up to the 2003 invasion of Iraq, senior members of the George W. Bush administration demonstrated their skill at influencing news coverage in ways that helped them ensure support for going to war.

Today, this may be changing. Digital media expert Taylor Owen writes:

> Where it used to be that the state had a virtual monopoly on the ability to shape the behavior of large numbers of people, this is no longer the case. Enabled by digital technology, disruptive innovators are now able to influence the behavior of large numbers of people without many of the societal constraints that have developed around state action.[18]

But who are these "disruptive innovators"? Many of them are well-meaning groups or individuals with important stories to tell, often based on first-hand knowledge. Now that they have direct access to audiences through new media, they may wield the same kind of influence – although more dispersed – that was once monopolized by governments, large news organizations, and other establishment information providers. Some of these innovators, however, are not so well-meaning, in the sense that in their devotion to a particular agenda they will opportunistically shape the information they provide, sometimes cutting corners on truthfulness.

If the new accessibility of media is to foster a healthy competition of ideas, an essential element will be a high level of transparency about sources' motivations and the origins of the information they are disseminating. The information consumer must decide whom to trust, an often difficult task when the internet is filled with websites and other venues whose true identity might not immediately be clear. News from the Middle East, for example, is provided by numerous online sources with neutral-sounding names that actually provide highly partisan versions of "news" from the region.

Social media, with their billions of content items, make discernment even more difficult. This abundance of sources means media literacy is especially important for the average news consumer as well as for diplomats and policymakers at all levels. A few news providers, such as the BBC or National Public Radio, might earn a high level of trust, but information with less certain origins particularly needs corroboration. There is no foolproof way to do this; checking a variety of sources that are reporting on the same issue or event is a logical approach, but it can be time-consuming and there is no way to know how many additional providers should be consulted.

Diplomats and others active in the international policy arena must navigate these treacherous waters. Adrian Monck of the World Economic Forum noted: "By giving a platform to anyone who wants to use it, social media has the potential to open and democratize societies. But social media can also create an illusion of community, diversity, power, and freedom. . . . Social media may give disproportionate exposure to radicalized voices."[19]

This is the risk-filled environment in which the twenty-first century diplomat must work. Along with challenges, there are opportunities. Canadian Foreign Minister John Baird observed: "We can engage in direct diplomacy, not just elite diplomacy. In the environment of instant communication and social media, we do have to move faster and not be afraid to try new things or make mistakes."[20]

## Connecting to the public

This environment in which diplomats must move quickly and take chances is made more complex by global publics that expect information to be delivered through various media and further assume that they are, at least to some extent, partners in the diplomatic process. Their growing expectations and clout mean that public diplomacy is increasingly integral to the future of diplomacy. The next chapter explores the expanding connections between governments and publics, and how this is affecting the future of diplomacy.

# 2

# The Rise of Public Diplomacy

Courting foreign publics has gone on as long as states have existed. The term "public diplomacy" was first used during the Cold War, when it was employed as a substitute for "propaganda," which had come to be seen as synonymous with "untruthful." It can be most easily defined in contrast with traditional diplomacy, which is government-to-government, while public diplomacy is government-to-public. It follows that the "public diplomat," who will be discussed below, is the diplomat who has expanded her or his purview to include connecting with various publics as well as officialdom.

This public dimension of diplomacy matters because to an unprecedented degree the public matters. A few countries – North Korea comes to mind – care little about what the rest of the world thinks of them. But most states compete with one another for foreign publics' approval. They want to be looked upon as leaders and hope their reputations will influence other nations' behavior. This is more than a popularity contest; backing for controversial policies may be at stake (as is noted in several examples in this chapter), and public opinion can affect international trade, education, and other matters.

A good formal definition of public diplomacy was published by the British Council in 1941 as its statement of purpose:

> The Council's aim is to create in a country overseas a basis of friendly knowledge and understanding of the people of this country, of their philosophy and way of life, which will lead to a sympathetic appreciation of British foreign policy.[1]

Responsibility for designing and implementing public diplomacy may be shared. Geoffrey Wiseman cites three options: "traditional," administered by a foreign affairs ministry; "whole of government," involving numerous government departments and agencies; and "new public diplomacy," which is conducted by governmental and non-governmental bodies. Wiseman notes that the assignment of responsibility depends on recognizing "when each approach – or combination of approaches – will be the most effective."[2]

Public diplomacy takes many forms. During the Cold War years, the United States and the Soviet Union fought battles for public opinion on many fronts. They relied on cultural envoys such as Louis Armstrong and the Bolshoi Ballet, and the United States also emphasized the work of the Peace Corps, which sent American volunteers into communities around the world.

Then, as now, much public diplomacy was media-centric. Throughout the Cold War, US and Soviet government broadcasters competed for the attention of audiences that had few alternative sources of information. Today, the media universe has expanded exponentially to include indigenous venues such as regional satellite broadcasting channels, Al Jazeera being among the best known. Add to these the internet-based media, particularly social media that allow and encourage people to gather information from a huge array of providers, and then talk to one another as they share the information and their opinions. The ability to choose from such an information smorgasbord makes more intense the competition for public opinion and loyalty, and in today's public diplomacy, success or failure is often determined by whom the public deems most credible.

In addition to its media projects, public diplomacy encompasses more personalized efforts undertaken by "public affairs officers," "public diplomacy specialists," or whatever a particular foreign ministry calls them. This role exists just in case people may occasionally be willing to look up from their mobile phone screens to talk with a real person.

Nations that want to wield global influence have no choice but to engage in public diplomacy. With the world's publics so thoroughly connected, they expect to be talked to and listened to, and they may push back when they perceive attempts at manipulation. The notion of people passively accepting communication is obsolete; new media encourage people to participate in debating issues that affect their lives. As R. S. Zaharna observes, today's publics constitute "an aggressive, digital-media-empowered audience that demands to know, 'Why wasn't I consulted?'" by policymakers of their own and other countries.[3]

Following the deceptive quiet of the first post-Cold War decade, public diplomacy became a focal point of foreign policy, especially for the United States, after the 2001 terrorist attacks. Americans were not only stunned by the attacks but also were perplexed by what they suddenly recognized as widespread antipathy toward their country, particularly in the Muslim world. The question widely asked by Americans was "Why do they hate us?"

Power attracts enemies, and during its time as the sole super-power, the perceived arrogance of the United States was a magnet for dissatisfaction. After the terrorist attacks, a military response was prepared immediately, targeting Al Qaeda's Afghanistan base of operations. To address anti-American sentiment, particularly in the Muslim world, US officials tapped one of the country's most-prized resources, the advertising industry, hoping for a quick fix of problems that had been festering for years. The task at hand proved more difficult than selling laundry detergent or fast food. The first product consisted of video messages, designed for broad-cast in Muslim countries around the world, showing Muslim Americans enjoying their lives in the United States. These "Happy Muslim" videos were so condescending that few Muslim countries would allow them to be aired.

This episode illustrates the failure of an essential part of public diplomacy: listening, which has been stressed by academics such as Nicholas Cull as one of the foundation stones of public diplo-macy. American policymakers were tone-deaf; they could not appreciate the level of resentment toward a superpower widely seen as irresponsible and disrespectful, particularly in its treat-ment of Palestinians and others in the Muslim world.

This might be an example of a public diplomacy effort that was more concerned with self-affirmation than with being in sync with foreign attitudes. Also, public diplomacy does not work well as a reactive tool. Rather than being initiated in response to a crisis, it should be used consistently to build long-term relationships that then may prove useful during difficult times.

More than a decade after the 2001 attacks, the United States and other countries are still trying to understand public diplomacy. They recognize that "soft power" – relying on attraction rather than coercion – is preferable to "hard power" measures such as military action and economic sanctions. Sometimes the situation does not allow an "either-or" choice. Although they may be searching for a third path, most nations' diplomats have yet to devise a workable formula for "smart power," a mix of soft and hard that appeals to global publics while advancing national interests. Part of the difficulty for policymakers who want to decide how to use public diplomacy is that they (and many others) are as yet unable to judge the still uncertain impact of a media revolution that has introduced unprecedented parity in access to information.

The response to the rise of the Islamic State has been an attempt to mix hard and soft: hard power on the battlefield, and soft power in efforts to disrupt IS recruiting. As of this writing, in mid-2015, following dual paths does not seem to be working well, perhaps because in this case both approaches have been poorly designed. Constrained by domestic and international political realities, the initial military plan had limited effect, and the IS soft power recruitment of young Muslims to help create a caliphate was not met by equally convincing counter-arguments.

Finding a way to offset the predisposition to rely on hard power may be the most significant challenge to public diplomacy in the years ahead. Strategists must put a hard edge on soft power; recognizing that public diplomacy will not be accepted as a legitimate diplomatic tool if it comprises only "nice" gestures that produce nothing more than ephemeral popularity. Public diplomacy must be grounded in discerning and meeting the needs of the publics to whom these efforts are directed, all as part of advancing the national interests of the diplomats' country.

There are reasons for enlisting political support from global publics. Particularly in this era of pervasive conversation on social media, influencing that discussion can pay off on matters ranging from winning support for one's foreign policies generally, to undermining the sentiments that nurture terrorism.

Without cultivation of public opinion through soft power methods, a nation's motives will be suspect, especially when hard power tactics are employed. In 2003, when the United States invaded Iraq, US credibility dropped so low that hardly any government or individual (other than many Americans) believed that the reasons for the war were anything other than the pursuit of Iraq's oil reserves and the vengeful desire to get rid of Saddam Hussein. The sympathetic goodwill that had accrued to the United States after the 2001 terrorist attacks had rapidly dissipated, in part because America's public diplomacy strategy had been narrowly conceived. Post-9/11 sympathy had opened doors, albeit briefly, even into countries such as Russia, but American public diplomacy did not significantly step across those thresholds. Instead, US policymakers' focus shifted to Iraq, and the perceived arrogance of power soon led to America being seen not as victim, but as oppressor.

The battering of the United States in world opinion spurred consideration by other countries about how they might use public diplomacy more effectively. Their approaches have varied, but they provide indications of what public diplomacy's role may be in the years ahead – a more integral part of foreign policy.

## China's cultural outreach

China is the world's most active practitioner of public diplomacy, devoting the equivalent of billions of US dollars to its efforts. Its emphasis on soft power is presumably based on recognition that for now, at least, China cannot match the United States in hard power capacity and so must take another path to assert itself as a superpower.

Just a few years ago, China's outreach, according to a US government analysis, consisted of little more than "a random scattering of a handful of pandas."[4] Today, however, China's public diplomacy features a panoply of programs, well-funded and large-scale. It has invested heavily in broadcasting and in providing economic development assistance to countries that can supply the natural resources China needs for growth and the locations where China can build trade and security networks. As for general visibility, hosting the 2008 Summer Olympics in Beijing and the 2010 World Expo in Shanghai proved successful at giving the world a look at China as a benign global presence. In 2022, China will again host the Olympics, this time the Winter Games, in and around Beijing.

Perhaps the most intriguing Chinese public diplomacy effort is its export of Chinese language and culture throughout the world through its Confucius Institutes. As of 2015, there were 475 institutes in 120 countries, with the largest concentrations in the United States, South Korea, and Japan, nations where "the China threat" is a political issue that China wants to defuse. The Chinese government's stated goal is to have a thousand institutes operating by 2020. Confucius Institutes outnumber similar projects of other countries, such as Germany's Goethe-Institut, which has 160 centers in 94 countries, and the United Kingdom's British Council, which has 70 centers in 49 countries.[5] The Confucius Institutes also differ from their counterparts in where they operate – they are mainly located on college and secondary school campuses – and in their financial support from their government. China has provided up to US$100,000 in matching funds to the local hosts of each of the institutes.

As with other nations' public diplomacy programs, the Confucius Institutes have a clear political purpose. Chinese Politburo member Li Changchun said that the institutes are "an important channel to glorify Chinese culture, to help Chinese culture spread to the world," which is "part of China's foreign propaganda strategy."[6]

Nothing surprising there, except perhaps the blunt honesty of the statement. Without doubt, the Confucius Institutes are designed to soften public opinion about China, presenting the country as a repository of admirable culture and diverting attention from the country's growing economic and military prowess.

In some cases, Confucius Institute funds have saved financially endangered Chinese-language programs and otherwise enhanced China-related offerings of the host country's educational institutions. The institutes have, however, also provoked pushback. In the United States, the American Association of University Professors criticized conditions imposed by some of the institutes located on American university campuses: "Confucius Institutes function as an arm of the Chinese state and are allowed to ignore academic freedom. ... Specifically, North American universities permit Confucius Institutes to advance a state agenda in the recruitment and control of academic staff, in the choice of curriculum, and in the restriction of debate."[7]

The lesson here is that even when a government's influence-building effort is dressed up as "public diplomacy" and is generously bankrolled, there are limits as to how much leeway it will be granted by the countries to which it is directed. The Chinese government may be able to exercise great control over its own population, but that might not work overseas. Successful public diplomacy depends in part on possessing a sophisticated understanding of the political psychology of other nations. China is still learning.

## Russia's broadcasting

The most visible tool of Russian public diplomacy is its television network, RT, formerly known by a less hip name, Russia Today. Its original channel, in English, began in 2005, and it has added Arabic- and Spanish-language channels since then, along with RT America and RT UK, which feature localized content. RT announced in late 2014 that its YouTube channels had garnered two billion views, more than CNN and Al Jazeera. Its companion service, Sputnik, provides news in 30 languages on radio and other media platforms.[8]

RT's production values are slick and its on-air personnel are television-smooth. Many of RT's stories are fundamentally accurate, but the overall coverage relentlessly reinforces the Russian government's worldview. A 2015 story about Western news reports discussed their focus on "Russia's so-called aggression in Ukraine," and an article about the US presidential campaign referred to a "political dung heap" of candidates. Positive stories about the West are rare. On the air and on its website, RT looks at news through a Putinesque lens, and mixes in opinion pieces such as "Regime Change in Russia? Think Again Neocons."

At first glance, this type of content seems to be a throwback to the Cold War, but it is carefully calibrated to have its desired effect on targeted audiences. *New Yorker* editor David Remnick has called RT "darkly, nastily brilliant, so much more sophisticated than Soviet propaganda."[9]

The Kremlin clearly believes RT is useful, providing it with an annual budget the equivalent of US$400 million (which is roughly twice the size of the Voice of America's budget).[10] The Russian government seems pleased with RT's provocative style, but like other broadcasters its overall effectiveness is questionable because it competes within an unprecedentedly crowded information environment. Even most of its regular viewers are almost certainly receiving information from additional sources, and this dilutes RT's impact. RT has also not been helped by well-publicized resignations of a few of its journalists who could no longer stomach the channel's purposely inaccurate reporting, such as about the conflict in Ukraine.

To counter RT and other Russian propaganda efforts, regional responses have been suggested. Among these are Ukraine Tomorrow, designed by the central government of that country, a channel in Estonia designed for the 25 percent of its population that speaks Russian as their first language, and a Lithuania-based pan-Baltic channel that is directed to that region's Russian-speaking minorities who are judged most susceptible to RT-type blandishments.[11]

For the past half-century, government broadcasting has been the dominant public diplomacy tool, with a handful of well-known networks such as the BBC, Deutsche Welle, the Voice of America, and others delivering news that reflected their respective governments' perspectives and their journalistic principles (even if these lack the self-aggrandizing flair of RT). Today, these channels are among the hundreds of satellite and cable broadcasters that offer news, religious programming, sports, and entertainment. Add to these the internet's array of information sources and the question arises, how much effort and money should be devoted to a single flagship channel?

Virtually every major broadcaster now provides an online as well as on-air product. Diplomatic policymakers must decide how best to compete with these offerings from other countries and with the expanding programming of commercial media industries. This will involve creating a large array of information venues targeted to particular audiences, rather than just focusing on one or a few broadcasting tools, as in the past. Online venues are particularly well suited for this diversity.

In many countries, such change will be complicated by domestic political considerations because the broadcasters have been around long enough to have both cultivated support and provoked opposition within their own governments. In the United States, to talk about changing anything related to Voice of America, for instance, will energize the broadcaster's allies and foes in Congress. They will rush to defend or attack, without paying much attention to the real issues related to the future of affecting global opinion through information dissemination.

"Information" in this context should be defined broadly. One of the world's most successful broadcasting enterprises is private, not governmental: Sesame Workshop, which reaches children around the globe with locally produced versions of Sesame Street and other educational activity. This work is especially valuable because there are also hate-filled broadcasts and online video messages directed at children. Given that public diplomacy should be forward-looking, more attention should be paid to young people. Sesame Workshop's local outsourcing for content and production could be a model for such efforts. Further, recognizing the web-savvy media-consuming habits of young people could allow constructing a public diplomacy framework with specialized online content. Cultivating today's young audiences might pay significant diplomatic dividends over the long term.

The era of traditional broadcasting-dominated public diplomacy has ended. The nations that want to emerge as globally influential in this arena must develop innovative strategies that will recognize how their audiences have changed in the ways they consume and use media, and must also take advantage of the many new methods available to reach these global publics.

## Israel's politicking

Israel considers itself to be in a precarious position. Its neighbors are, to varying degrees, hostile, and its relationships with the countries of Western Europe are up and down. On the other hand, it has a vibrant economy and a solid national identity among its Jewish population, which is about 75 percent of the country's total.

Israel's public diplomacy, like that of many other nations, is aimed at creating a generally positive image for the country, which can help attract investment and win admirers who might, in their own countries, aid in addressing Israel's security concerns. Israel also tries to influence specific political positions of other countries. This often centers on measures before the United Nations or national governments concerning Palestinian-related issues or security questions regarding nearby states. Israel relies heavily on the Jewish diaspora, the largest concentration of which (almost the size of the Jewish population of Israel itself) is found in the United States. More broadly, Israel counts on supportive Americans – by no means all of them Jewish – to help represent and advance Israel's interests.

The US government has been friendly to Israel since its founding in 1948, but on occasions the two countries have been at loggerheads. No dispute has been more fractious than that surrounding the 2015 international agreement on Iran's nuclear capacity. Brokered primarily by the United States, this agreement was seen by Israel as an insufficient deterrent to Iran's ability to develop nuclear weapons. Israel and its proxies intervened in America's highly partisan politics to try to derail the deal by generating public pressure on Congress to vote against what the Obama administration considered a significant diplomatic achievement.

Israeli efforts on this issue were impossible to avoid, albeit they were sometimes indirect. Pro-Israel organizations, which usually deny any formal connection to the Israeli government, purchased advertisements attacking the agreement as a danger not only to Israel, but also to the United States itself. These groups mobilized supporters to argue the anti-agreement case to elected officials and opinion leaders.

The American Israel Public Affairs Committee (AIPAC) was at the forefront of this effort. With more than 100,000 members and 17 regional offices, AIPAC has supporters in every congressional district, and among these are financial contributors to political candidates of both parties.[12] In its ability to quickly galvanize congressional support, AIPAC is recognized as one of the top lobbying groups in the country. AIPAC denies that it operates at the behest of the Israeli government, but the ties are close, even if not formal.

Relying heavily on social media and other internet presence, Israeli diplomatic missions in the United States delivered a steady stream of messaging such as the "Iran Deal Bulletin," which was sent by email several times each week to large lists of recipients. More directly, Israeli Prime Minister Benjamin Netanyahu accepted an invitation from the Republican Speaker of the House of Representatives to address a joint session of Congress. This was done without informing the White House, a clear breach of diplomatic protocol that infuriated even some of Israel's staunch American supporters.

This effort was public diplomacy at a rare level of intensity. In terms of reaching a big audience, the Israeli campaign was successful, reflecting sophisticated planning on the Israelis' part. But before this approach is adopted by others as a model for public diplomacy related to security, trade, and other issues, it is worth considering whether such efforts may be perceived as inappropriate meddling and thus prove counterproductive. The message of this campaign, whether stated or implicit, was, "Urge the US Congress to vote against the Obama administration's diplomacy." There were plenty of members of Congress who agreed with that, some on purely partisan grounds and others thinking that Iran was untrustworthy and that a continuation of economic sanctions might produce a better deal. Some were not averse to taking military action to try to destroy Iran's nuclear facilities.

All that is part of legitimate debate within the US political system. But does a foreign government have any business jumping into such a debate as wholeheartedly as Israel did?

The Israeli campaign could be seen as classic public diplomacy – a government reaching out directly to a foreign public – or it could be seen as inappropriate interference likely to produce an anti-Israel backlash.

This is a line public diplomats should be wary about crossing. Even in the world of hardboiled foreign affairs, subtlety and restraint have value. For Israel, the results of its political activity could prove damaging. Numerous Western European countries have backed away from Israel due to that country's policies toward Palestinians, and jeopardizing broad-based American support could mean even greater isolation of Israel.

Of course, it can be argued that by definition public diplomacy involves interfering in another nation's internal affairs. After all, it is direct outreach to a foreign population. This may be more problematic when the two countries are allies and diplomatic etiquette calls for better behavior. When the stakes are high enough, however, as Israel considered them to be in relation to the Iran agreement, etiquette might be set aside. That could have lingering diplomatic consequences.

## The United States' grass roots outreach

The United States is active in public diplomacy in many ways: broadcasting, online connections, cultural and student exchanges, economic assistance, and more, with growing emphasis on high-tech ventures such as the @america Center located in a Jakarta shopping mall, where young Indonesians gather to use

US government computers and soak up information about the United States. Clearly, the United States, like many other nations, is moving toward greater emphasis on such up-to-date tools. But let's consider a retro example – one begun a half-century ago – and see if it offers lessons valid for the future.

In 1961, a few weeks into his presidency, John F. Kennedy signed an executive order creating the Peace Corps, which would deploy volunteers to bring American know-how and values to cities and villages where the contests of the Cold War were near the surface of daily life. In an accompanying statement, Kennedy said: "We will only send abroad Americans who are wanted by the host country – who have a real job to do – and who are qualified to do that job."[13]

Over the years, the Peace Corps has established an impressive track record. As of 2015, 220,000 volunteers had served in 140 countries, with most volunteers working in Africa and Latin America. In fiscal year 2014, the Peace Corps budget was $379 million.[14] Although no longer as visible as it had been when the Kennedy "New Frontier" cachet meant something, it has become an enduring part of American diplomacy and volunteerism, and evidence that superpower foreign policy and low-key altruism can be compatible.

Questions arise, however, about the twenty-first-century relevance of the Peace Corps. Development expert Charles Kenny asked, "In an age of globe-trotting American college kids, ubiquitous internet access, and mobile phone networks that reach even sub-Saharan cattle herders, does the world still need the Peace Corps?"[15] A response to that question requires determining the value of retaining on-the-ground, in-person contacts as one facet of public diplomacy. A temptation exists to turn over interpersonal relationships to social media, which would cost far less than training and deploying volunteers. But does the intangible asset of being represented by a real person make such costs worthwhile?

The presumed value of one-to-one connection can be seen today in the US government's commitment to fostering entrepreneurship in parts of the world that need enhanced economic development. During his trip to Kenya in 2015, President Obama and Kenya's President Uhuru Kenyatta jointly opened the Global Entrepreneurship Summit at which Obama announced private sector and US government pledges of more than US$1 billion in support of projects initiated by young people and women. Spin-offs from the summit include science and technology boot camps for start-ups, training in life skills as well as business skills, and other programs that bring government and private sector expertise to people who have imagination and energy and just need a boost to build the momentum they require.[16]

At the heart of many of these efforts is mentorship provided by business people from the United States and elsewhere who work directly with the aspiring entrepreneurs. Muslim countries, where US public diplomacy has struggled to gain traction, receive particular attention in this program. The concept is not far removed from the Peace Corps's methods of working directly within communities. To be sure, these business start-ups also rely on email, websites, and other internet tools, but personal connections are at the heart of the entrepreneurship effort.

This updated version of the Peace Corps approach to public diplomacy illustrates the value of using micro tactics to reach macro outcomes. Entrepreneurship can improve lives of individuals and communities in ways that reflect goals that, although tech-oriented, are similar to those of the Peace Corps. It might be that the public diplomacy of the future would benefit from occasionally reaching back into the past and reconstituting the personalized idealism of the Peace Corps.

# Tomorrow's public diplomacy

## Credibility

Skepticism is a good thing generally, especially when evaluating the information that bombards us electronically from so many directions. Most information providers have ulterior motives – financial, political, or something else. Information is imbued with biases; sometimes intentional, sometimes not. The public that receives information also is affected by its own biases, and that audience will often seek out information sources considered like-minded and therefore credible. An example: the popularity of Al Jazeera during its early years.

Born in 1996 and well-funded by the government of Qatar, Al Jazeera understood its audience. It provided relatively compre-hensive newscasts and lively talk shows, its production values rivaled those of the big Western channels such as the BBC and CNN, and it was a clear upgrade from the stodgy, tightly controlled news programming in most other Arab states. Most important, its biases were those of its audience. When it reported the Intifada of 2000, it did so with a clear pro-Palestinian slant, which meshed perfectly with the views of most of its viewers. For the first time, the Arab audience was seeing news about Arabs reported by Arabs; "We are seeing our lives through our own eyes."

This might not be "good journalism" according to Western standards of being dispassionate and objective, but it quickly won a large and loyal audience because in its viewers' eyes it was *credible*. Al Jazeera was trusted by many Arabs because it was "ours."

Meeting the need for credibility requires care on the part of public diplomats – those who design and those who implement public diplomacy. In many cases they will face a barrier of suspicion and must find a way to circumvent it. Doing so requires choosing the appropriate voice for reaching the targeted public. Another example from the Arab world: soon after the 2001 attacks, the US government created Arabic-language broadcasters, the Al Hurra television channels and Radio Sawa. Hundreds of millions of dollars were spent on these ventures, but they achieved only limited success. Sawa attracted listeners because it broadcast a mix of Western and Middle Eastern music interspersed with pro-American newscasts (many in the audience listened to the former and switched off the latter), but Al Hurra struggled. It was known to be physically based in a suburb of Washington, DC, its on-air personnel had little affinity with the audience, and it avoided covering stories in which its audience was interested but offended the political sensibilities of US officials. For example, during those years, perhaps the most popular political figure in the Arab world was Hassan Nasrallah, the head of Hezbollah. If he gave a major speech, Arab broadcasters would cover it heavily, but if Al Hurra did so, the channel's managers would be severely criticized by Congress. And if Al Hurra did not cover it, the audience would find it elsewhere.

Al Hurra devoted itself to coverage its targeted viewers could easily ignore. It never acquired the credibility it needed to attract and hold a sizable audience. Some critics of the US broadcasting efforts suggested relying instead on "public diplomacy by proxy": persistent, carefully organized appearances by US officials on Arab channels such as Al Jazeera. The officials might undergo some rough questioning, but they would reach many viewers, and because they were on the Arab channels trusted by the audience, these viewers would be more likely to pay attention to what was being said.

This proxy approach is not new; the British government in 1940–1 relied heavily on UK-based American journalists, rather than just the BBC, to deliver information that helped pull the United States away from isolationism and toward substantive support for Britain's war effort. For a US audience, the American correspondents were judged to be more credible than Britain's own news media. This effort was an important factor in the evolution of American public opinion at that time.

As this example indicates, a crucial question related to credibility is, "Who should be the messenger?" With so many information delivery vehicles available, options are many. Sometimes, unfortunately, hubris gets in the way of sensible decision making, and ownership is judged more important than effectiveness. But global audiences are becoming more stringent in deciding whom to trust, and so no country's public diplomacy planners may take credibility for granted.

## Speed

As with other aspects of diplomacy, public diplomacy's future will be shaped in part by the speed at which information moves. Public diplomacy practitioners have little choice but to match this pace; like it or not, they must keep up with the rest of the world.

As a result, addressing "What shall we say?" often takes precedence over "What shall we do?" Words race ahead of policy. In response to a crisis or just to parry another country's pronouncement, so much pressure exists to produce a tweet or other message almost instantly that broad strategy may be pushed aside in favor of a quick online tactical maneuver. Foreign ministries are devising internal rules for this process: Who in an embassy should be authorized to tweet officially? Should there be a vetting procedure? Should an initial response be backed up with a more elaborate statement? How can our response be crafted so it will stand out in the vast crowd of online traffic?

The question that does *not* seem to often be asked is, "Why can't we slow down and think this through?" Most issues can be addressed tomorrow better than today. Granted, there are true crises that require instant action and delaying can exacerbate these situations. When the infamous *Innocence of Muslims* video appeared on YouTube and its existence was widely reported by various media, mobs began to form and US diplomatic outposts were endangered. An effort to tamp down the anger and disassociate the American government from the video had to be undertaken immediately. But such situations are rare. If a foreign government official makes a snarky comment online, responding rapidly in kind might make matters worse. Just because they are available, instant communication tools do not always require instant use.

The acceleration of diplomatic activity has been continuous, with the pace being set by the latest technological advances. The advent of 24-hour, all-news television channels put pressure on policymakers to feed the beast's insatiable appetite for content, but sometimes that appetite can work to a government's advantage. All-news channels require large amounts of material, and so instead of covering a government news conference and chopping it down to a minute or two in an edited news report, an all-news provider might cover the entire event live. No editing; the government can say what it wants and reach the public directly. (This "Eureka moment" for government officials was first noticeable during CNN's coverage of the 1991 Gulf War when the Pentagon took full advantage of the network's hunger for live content and provided hours-long briefings that were delivered to the audience in their long-winded entirety.)

This raises journalistic issues about live coverage being merely an information conveyor belt to the public without editorial intervention. From diplomats' standpoint, however, it presents an opportunity to at least temporarily control the message that reaches the public. That is also the allure of Twitter and other instant contact tools: no need for an interlocutor such as a news organization.

Going live today, however, is far different from when a few 24-hour news channels dominated real-time information dissemination. Send a tweet or post a YouTube video and you drop your message into a cauldron of voices and images. Most of these are irrelevant to whatever you are addressing, but you are likely to stir up at least some responses, both supportive and hostile. You can ignore these, delivering your message and walking away, but doing so cedes control of the continuing conversation to others. Once the online back-and-forth begins and new parties jump in, the discussion may take on a life of its own, so this kind of engagement should not be entered into without a strategy for participation and anticipating where it might lead.

Speed has changed the culture of diplomacy. The more that new technologies are relied upon, the more that diplomacy's traditionally deliberate pace is seen as archaic, particularly by publics accustomed to getting information NOW about matters that affect them. Diplomacy has always adjusted to changes in the professional culture within which it operates, and today it has no choice but to keep doing so . . . and quickly.

## Scope

To whom should diplomats listen and to whom should they reach out? Listening is a crucial element of public diplomacy, but the level of chatter, particularly on the internet, is such that not every voice – no matter how insistent – can be accorded the same level of attention. The general clamor is amplified by social media, and those engaged in public diplomacy must assign priorities to those voices most worth listening to.

Today, "official channels" constitute just a small fraction of the communication venues to which diplomats must be attentive. The diplomatic pouch might still be available, but the back-and-forth among diplomats more often relies on the instantaneous exchanges allowed by new media. As practitioners of public diplomacy themselves, world leaders have found Twitter to be a particularly convenient way to send brief messages to the news media and the public. As of 2015, the top three world leaders in terms of Twitter followers were President Barack Obama, Pope Francis, and Indian Prime Minister Narendra Modi. As for influence, however, Pope Francis was at the top of the list in 2015 because each of his tweets averaged nearly 10,000 retweets, while President Obama's tweets were retweeted only about 1,200 times. Among diplomats in 2015, more than 4,100 diplomatic missions and ambassadors used Twitter.[17]

As for broader communication with interest groups and individuals – there are only so many hours in a day. The volume of incoming emails, not to mention all the indirect communication such as news broadcasts that must be monitored, is enormous.

Think about the daily Facebook postings, Twitter tweets, YouTube videos, content from Instagram, Pinterest, and on and on. Numbering more than a billion items each day, most of this content is irrelevant, but bits and pieces are vitally important. Terrorist organizations, for instance, use internet communication to maintain their networks – recruiting, fundraising, training, and more, including perhaps signaling their future activity.

Intelligence agencies have developed sophisticated "spiders" that can crawl through the web's massive amounts of electronic material, looking for and indexing keywords. Telephonic communication is similarly scanned. After the 2001 terrorist attacks, the Central Intelligence Agency provided seed money to tech firms to work on such matters. Some of the resulting systems can read large numbers of files in a database, capturing metadata and finding links between individuals and organizations. This kind of system can also give "sentiment scores" to certain words to help detect emotion and can identify code words.[18]

Diplomats need something comparable and with a sorting capacity that tech wizards can presumably design. While intelligence agencies may be particularly concerned about detecting threats, diplomats need to understand more general global conversation about issues. Policymakers require something sophisticated that shows how the words are used. Context matters, and nuance remains important in the language of diplomacy. Such things defy quantification. Perhaps most needed is a daily (or, during a crisis, a constant) overview of social media content as it relates to current policy-related matters. Ideally, at least some of this content could be tracked by country of origin and other identifiers.

Reaping the rewards of listening requires doing so in a comprehensive and timely way. Long past are the days when this could be accomplished by simply scanning newspapers or news broadcasts from around the world, although that still has value.

One result of listening should be outreach, and again the challenge is determining to whom and how. The audience interested in foreign policy matters can no longer be assumed to be an easily identifiable elite. That assumption once seemed logical because mass constituencies for issues could rarely make themselves heard. But they exist, often seething and occasionally erupting.

Recent examples of this include the Arab uprisings of early 2011 and the global "Occupy" movement that appeared a few months later. Both were unanticipated by policymakers and both, at least initially, were beyond the reach of the diplomatic community's information-gathering capacity. These were political phenomena that relied heavily on social media to state their aims and communicate internally and externally. Such movements are likely to appear again, using new media even more adroitly, and it would be foolish for governments and their diplomats to remain uncommunicative in response to the mobilization of millions of people.

No political action is spontaneous; the observant can detect causes and identify activists before they appear in the news media's spotlight. So why were responses to "Arab spring" and "Occupy" so ragged? Diplomacy has long been plagued by uninformed or belated judgment in such matters, sometimes by remote policymakers and sometimes by people close to the action, but essential information is usually accessible by the attentive. Organizers of the Arab spring uprising in Egypt relied heavily on Facebook and other social media to handle logistics of protests and mobilize supporters. The movement's initial success would have been less surprising to policymakers if this social media content had been watched more carefully.

The political dynamics of the twenty-first century will reflect the good and the bad aspects of the enhanced ability to collect information. "Identification and monitoring" may improve decision making, but they can also constrain political freedom. Law and ethics must keep pace if new methods of information-gathering are not to become tools of oppression.

At the heart of the redefined scope of listening and outreach should be recognition that diplomacy must become more inclusive. The elites who long dominated the closed world of diplomacy now share access to policymakers with the publics that have been given voice by new media tools. In that egalitarian expansion is the essence of the diplomacy of the future.

## Results

When can public diplomacy be judged successful? What proof is available? Such are the questions raised by critics of public diplomacy – those who think the money spent on public diplomacy would better be devoted to weapons procurement or other "real" ways of dealing with the rest of the world.

Coming up with proof of public diplomacy's accomplishments can be challenging. Consider the 19-year-old who comes to your country for a year in an academic exchange program that is part of your public diplomacy. The young woman has a good experience and returns home with positive thoughts about your country. How are the effects of that measured? Now suppose that 30 years later she becomes her nation's prime minister, and her policy toward your country is strongly influenced, in a positive way, by her experience in that exchange program.

That is a public diplomacy success, but 30 years have passed before this result could be seen. Unlike acquiring a jet fighter loaded with missiles, public diplomacy is a slow, incremental process. Unlike the elements of modern diplomacy that are so profoundly affected by demands for high-speed action, the seeds planted by exchange programs and the like take time to germinate and produce a crop. But many of those who control governmental purse strings like to pound the table and demand *results*, meaning something quantifiable and immediate.

It should be noted that exchange programs do not always produce positive outcomes. There are cases such as that of Sayyid Qutb, an early theoretician of Egypt's Muslim Brotherhood, who as a student in Colorado in 1949 was repelled by what he perceived as pervasive licentiousness in American life. He returned to Egypt more radicalized than he had been when he began his trip.[19]

The difficulties in evaluating exchange programs extend across most public diplomacy projects. US diplomat Robert Banks wrote: "It is often difficult to draw a straight line of causation between a public diplomacy program and its desired result. Time, external events, and other actors can intervene to complicate the cause-effect equation."[20]

Formal evaluation is difficult because determining metrics for this field is an inexact task. Public diplomacy also challenges evaluators because it is not always clear what it is supposed to do. "Winning hearts and minds" is sometimes cited, although that expression remains colored by self-delusional aspects of the Vietnam War, when it was frequently used. Further, as with evaluation of most things, numbers might mean less than they seem to. Suppose the government of France arranges a series of five concerts by one of France's premier orchestras in Country X. The concerts attract large audiences and much favorable publicity. What does that do for France? Unless sophisticated (and expensive) public opinion research accompanies the concerts, determining the public diplomacy value of the concerts will be mostly a matter of guesswork.

Common sense should tell the French government that based on audience size it has benefitted from the positive attention the concerts received, but policymakers may want the benefit substantiated by solid "proof." Demanding such evidence reflects a misunderstanding of the effects of public diplomacy. They are incremental. The orchestra should go back to Country X next year, and then the year after that. Over time, France will seem more familiar to citizens of X and, assuming there are no intervening negative factors that would undermine the public diplomacy, France would have a net gain of trust.

Of course, there must be a reason for courting Country X in the first place. That is what needs evaluating. Expansion of trade? A new security agreement? Support for France in some international forum? Are those important and realistic goals?

Public diplomacy is pointless if it is free-standing, separate from defined foreign policy objectives. In that case, it would be just smiles and gifts, and it would deserve the skepticism of policymakers and funders. It would also deserve the skepticism of the public diplomats themselves. As they develop new programs and refine existing ones, they need data.

This underscores the challenge facing advocates of public diplomacy. They must prove, as best they can, why it matters, and by extension, why foreign publics matter. This takes us back to communication; global publics will continue to use new media tools to pull themselves into conversations that affect them from which they were previously excluded. Diplomacy's future will depend in part on the ability to adjust and incorporate these publics in the making and implementation of foreign policy.

As the next chapter illustrates, the support of global publics is sought not just by nations, but also by non-state actors. Ranging from international humanitarian organizations to terrorist groups, non-state actors are joining traditional players in making their presence felt within the world of diplomacy.

# 3

# States and Non-States

Part of the diplomat's job is to engage in negotiation on behalf of one's nation or cause. Alliances are forged, trade agreements built, conflicts prevented or brought to an end, and generally the interests of states are individually advanced and collectively balanced, with diplomats making the best of the circumstances in which they find themselves.

Traditionally, diplomats have been the agents of states and, more recently, of international organizations. The modern state is an offspring of the Peace of Westphalia of 1648, which formalized the notion of "sovereignty": acceptance of the idea that the state would be ruled by its own sovereign rather than being a piece of an empire; that the state would be free to select its established religion; and perhaps most important, that sovereigns should mind their own business, and no state should interfere in the affairs of another. That has turned out to be, in many cases, more an ideal than reality.

For the most part, diplomats' clients - their states - have been political entities with physical definition, their borders identifiable on maps and their political structures given validity by popular will or compulsion. Sometimes a state's existence could be the subject of diplomacy, as when negotiations led to "Germany" (as the German Empire) coming into existence in 1871 by gathering Prussia and other German states into a newly formalized amalgamation.

When interstate, as opposed to civil, wars erupted, protagonists were usually clearly identified, as were the goals of the parties of the conflict. These goals were usually to batter the opponent into submission and seize or receive by surrender the opponent's territory and other assets. During the Second World War, the major Allied powers – the United States, the United Kingdom, and the Soviet Union – trained their wrath and firepower on other states, primarily Germany and Japan. The enemy had a defined physical existence that could be targeted. In this instance, diplomacy was pushed aside; the Allied warriors demanded unconditional surrender.

Jump forward to the beginning of the twenty-first century and note how this has changed in some instances. We speak of "failed states" and "non-state actors" that are more relevant to prospects for global stability than are many conventional states. As of mid-2015, the most notable, and notorious, failed state is Syria. There is still a central government, but central in name only. It controls only a small portion of what just four years earlier had been a relatively cohesive entity. Diplomats could still talk with that government and its leader, President Bashar Assad, as happened when, in 2013 at the instigation of the United States and Russia, Assad made a deal to surrender his regime's chemical weapons. But that was an exception, as it was clear that much of what had been Syria, including its largest city, Aleppo, was outside the regime's control.

This was not a case of another recognized state invading Syria and seizing its territory, and it was more complicated than a civil war. The combatants included a quasi-state that called itself the Islamic State and a non-state, Al Qaeda, which operated in Syria as the Al-Nusra Front. Also among the dozens of groups of fighters opposed to the Assad regime were Kurds from a virtual state of "Kurdistan," which comprised sizable populations in Iraq and Turkey, as well as Syria. "Kurdistan" is not formally recognized as a state by the United Nations or other international bodies, but it is a significant player in Middle Eastern affairs.

The Kurds are best organized in Iraq, where they enjoy semi-autonomous status granted by the flimsy Iraqi government and have their own *Peshmerga* military force, which has been deployed into Kurdish areas in Syria as well as Iraq. The Kurds also have de facto embassies in numerous nations.

Despite the Iraqi Kurds edging toward formal nationhood, most of these active non-states exist outside the realm of traditional diplomacy. IS and Al Qaeda behave in such reprehensible ways that negotiating with them has, at least so far, been inconceivable. And yet, they cannot be ignored. Al Qaeda had the wherewithal to attack the United States, and IS was able to take and hold (for who knows how long) significant amounts of territory.

Although neither IS nor Al Qaeda engages in conventional diplomacy, those who align against them rely on diplomacy to build coalitions that can employ effective military and political countermeasures.

Al Qaeda had attacked the most powerful nation on the planet, killed thousands of its citizens, and then – even after taking heavy casualties inflicted by invading US forces and their Afghan partners – its remnants were able to slip away into Pakistan. Diplomats could construct alliances to fight Al Qaeda, but beyond that, they hit a brick wall. Invading Afghanistan was one thing; pursuing Al Qaeda into Pakistan would be very different, infringing on the sovereignty of a "friendly" state and disrupting a delicate regional power structure. The struggle against Al Qaeda would be determined on scattered battlefields and through covert special operations, not at a negotiating table. Diplomacy was limited to the building of anti-Al Qaeda alliances. There would be no diplomatic end to this conflict; diplomacy has its limits.

## Ancient history: the Cold War

To appreciate how much the role of diplomacy had changed, look back just a few decades. For those who like their global politics easy to understand, the Cold War was ideal. Two superpowers, the United States and the Soviet Union, dominated the world. Many other countries were friends of one or the other, or tried to remain outside the fray. They all watched as the two giants pawed the earth and snorted. The center of the universe was Europe, where members of NATO and the Warsaw Pact eyed each other warily across numerous borders. Stockpiles of conventional and nuclear weapons grew ever fatter, gorged on spending that no one could afford. The looming menace in this face-off was MAD – Mutually Assured Destruction.

Occasionally, as during the Cuban Missile Crisis of 1962, the most lethal of this weaponry came frighteningly close to being used. Diplomacy, however, prevailed. US President John Kennedy and Soviet Premier Nikita Khrushchev were the principals, but ambassadors and other diplomats were important supporting players, the United Nations was a valuable forum, and even a television correspondent was pressed into duty as a diplomatic messenger. In this instance, shrewd leadership combined with good luck to ensure that diplomacy prevailed and the Cold War stayed cold.

Until the Soviet Union disintegrated in 1991, superpower diplomacy played out like a high-stakes chess game. The two principal protagonists each had allies and assorted proxies. Some countries, such as India, proclaimed themselves "non-aligned" and thereby open to courtship (the more lavish the better). The Soviet Union made certain its "allies" stayed in line, using its military to crush disobedience in Hungary, Czechoslovakia, and elsewhere. The United States used overt and covert tactics to advance its purported interests in numerous countries. Localized wars broke out in Africa, Latin America, and Southeast Asia, but even in these instances the fingerprints of the two major powers were easily detected. No one had clean hands.

## Everybody's century

Throughout all this, diplomats almost always knew with whom they were dealing. Superpowers, their proxies, and international organizations such as the United Nations sometimes tripped over one another, but even amidst disorder the Westphalian system more or less held together.

Once the Cold War ended and the Soviet Union dissolved, the bipolar power structure briefly became unipolar, with the United

States at the top. But that didn't last long. The rise of China and regional economic powers such as the European Union, plus emerging "tigers" in Asia, Latin America, and Africa contributed to a more horizontal array of influential players. Throughout this transformation, diplomacy not only retained much of its traditional role but also, in the absence of superpower military tension, became more robust. The United States negotiated with China, Russia alternately cajoled and bullied its near neighbors, countries in South America and elsewhere crafted trade deals, the European Union reshaped relationships in its region, and so on. Business as usual; diplomats went about their work.

It didn't take long for the twenty-first century to become a showcase for transition. Throughout the late 1990s, the internet gained traction as an essential part of life, at least in the most developed countries. Then the attack on the United States in 2001 and terrorist outrages in London, Madrid, and elsewhere signaled important changes in world order. Although none of these attacks involved weapons of mass destruction – chemical, biological, or nuclear – it was certainly conceivable that a non-state actor such as Al Qaeda could buy, steal, or create for itself the same kind of weapon that was once solely in the possession of major powers.

Meanwhile, diplomats were dealing with shifts in the ranks of the traditional powers and those countries that aspired to join their ranks. Among these were those whose leaders thought that even if the twentieth century had been the "American century," the twenty-first should see the deck reshuffled.

The United States, however, was not inclined to fade into the background, although some of its policy experts recognized that a changed outlook was essential. Joseph Nye wrote: "If the American Century is to continue, it will not be enough to think in terms of America's power *over* others. One must also think in terms of power to accomplish joint goals, which involves power *with* others."[1] Further, observed Nye, power diffusion, rather than power transmission, was becoming central. This involves national narratives that attract others. Nye noted, "Conventional wisdom has always held that the government with the largest military prevails, but in an information age it may be the state (or non-states) with the best story that wins."[2]

If Nye's diagnosis of power is correct, the work of the diplomat must change accordingly. Traditionally, the diplomat was a personalization of his or her country's strength: military, economic, cultural. During the Cold War, US and Soviet diplomats were therefore the most formidable in dealings with other states. They represented hard power, which their two countries largely monopolized. But if brains as well as muscle are recognized, new players move into leadership roles. Singapore, Brazil, Nigeria, and others have high aspirations and the potential to achieve them. Their diplomats' actions reflect the stories of these rising nations.

## Non-state actors

Dealing with the non-state actors in this mix is more problematic. Again, media tools serve as equalizers, giving these international actors greater credibility and more access to global publics than they may have had in the past. But what does that mean in terms of diplomacy? At what point does a quasi-state cross a threshold into becoming a state, or at least taking on de facto legitimacy? Can it achieve this simply by declaring itself to be a state of sorts?

IS declared that the territory it had seized in Syria and Iraq constituted a new Muslim caliphate, and it took steps to ensure that this was more than an unsupported proclamation. A *New York Times* report in June 2015 stated that IS was "offering reliable, if harsh, security; providing jobs in decimated economies; and projecting a rare sense of order in a region overwhelmed by conflict." Further, the report noted, IS "has millions of people under its charge, as well as archaeological sites, a hydroelectric dam, and oil fields that help finance its operations."[3]

An additional *New York Times* story contended that as IS holds the territory it has seized and builds its capacity to govern, "the group is transforming into a functioning state that uses extreme violence – terror – as a tool." IS is not the first to do this, and it may succeed because it "has provided relative stability in a region troubled by war and chaos while filling a vacuum left by failing and corrupt governments that also employed violence – arrest, torture, and detention."[4] Of course, IS itself relies on arrest, torture, and detention, and the "stability" it claims is built on oppression, which over time contributes to *instability*. There is no sense in trying to clothe IS in respectability; the clothing won't fit.

The Islamic State more or less follows the model of the Taliban, which governed much of Afghanistan from September 1996 until December 2001, when it was driven from power by its opponents within Afghanistan, heavily supported by US forces. Like IS, the Taliban provided security and services, enforcing its rule harshly. It was officially recognized as the government of Afghanistan by only three countries: Saudi Arabia, Pakistan, and the United Arab Emirates. (The United Nations and some countries recognized an Afghan opposition coalition led by the Northern Alliance.)

The Taliban took control of an existing state, while IS defines its new state based on the territory it can seize and administer.

Suppose the military efforts orchestrated by the United States and others prove insufficient to dislodge IS and it continues to control a large area and population; what should happen next? Stephen M. Walt observed:

> If the Islamic State manages to cling to power, consolidate its position, and create a genuine de facto state in what was previously part of Iraq and Syria, then other states will need to work together to teach it the facts of life in the international system. And because the Islamic State is not in fact that powerful, preventing it from expanding or increasing its power and imposing costs for its abhorrent behavior should not be all that hard.[5]

If the "abhorrent behavior" that has characterized IS is moderated (or becomes less visible) and the new "state" becomes geographically entrenched, other nations may need to decide how to deal with it in non-military ways unless they become willing to deploy a large ground force and commit to war on a far larger scale. Particularly given the politico-religious dynamics of the region, this Sunni entity, if viable, would have strategic influence that regional and global powers could not ignore. As this is written, IS's propensity to showcase beheadings and other horrid acts makes this seem unlikely, but IS's leadership has proved itself to be shrewd and adaptable. As morally reprehensible as dealing with IS may be, at some point its regional influence might make necessary a diplomatic strategy to complement the military one. It wouldn't be the first time that diplomats have had to confront evil, swallow hard, and at least temporarily treat the beast as human.

If IS is not defeated on the battlefield, it will derive strength from the weakness of those countries in which it has implanted itself. The fantasy of a unified Iraq will continue to unravel, allowing IS to be a malign "Sunnistan," while Shias in the area gather within their own state, be it called "Iraq" or something else. Nearby, the part of "Kurdistan" within Iraq will gain political traction as a relatively stable island amidst chaos and conflict. Kurdistan, however, would immediately become problematic for Turkey and Iran, which have their own Kurdish populations that might want to secede and join their kin in their own state. Given Turkey's role in NATO and Iran's strategic significance, diplomats would need to work overtime to ensure that Kurd-centered conflicts did not erupt.

All this is relevant to the future of diplomacy because it illustrates how the geopolitics of the world shift, sometimes with a slight trembling, sometimes in a major earthquake. Diplomats individually and the institutions for which they work must be able to adapt to instability and make decisions that are both principled and pragmatic. In the Kurds' situation, for instance, should "Kurdistan" be diplomatically recognized and should it be invited to join the United Nations? The Kurds have been oppressed for centuries and yet still hold on to their identity. They have fought fiercely against Saddam Hussein, IS, and others. Their case is strong, but perhaps not strong enough for other countries to recognize their state and so earn the displeasure of Turkey and Iran.

Even nomenclature can pose a diplomatic challenge. IS prefers to refer to itself as the "Islamic State." That offends many Muslims who find its bloody activities repulsive. Nevertheless, many news organizations, such as the BBC, use "Islamic State" because that is what the group chooses to call itself. British Prime Minister David Cameron jumped in and said, "I wish the BBC would stop calling it 'Islamic State' because it is not an Islamic state." Cameron wanted to deny the group any trappings of religious or statehood legitimacy. The BBC declined to make the change, saying that doing so would open the door to constantly making value judgments and impairing impartiality.[6]

Dealing with the various parties in the remnants of Syria and Iraq will challenge diplomats' skill and conscience. There are few, if any, "good guys" in this war, just players from near and far, and millions of victims. As we watch diplomats weave their way through the complexities of this conflict, it is worth remembering that diplomacy and morality have often had an uneasy relationship. History is full of examples of democracies cuddling with tyrants in order to advance security or economic interests. In such cases, diplomats might try to alter policy with which they disagree. But diplomats are agents, and their job is to attain objectives determined by those who make policy. In some cases that task may collide with conscience, and the individual diplomat – a person, not a machine – may face a choice between carrying on or resigning.

The Middle East provides many examples of the dystopian morass in which diplomats often must operate, but the world of non-state actors also comprises organizations engaged in beneficial work. Aided by new communication technologies, they are able to mount a substantial, visible presence and so have a better chance than in the past to affect policy.

Consider Medecins Sans Frontieres (MSF), or Doctors Without Borders, the emergency medical response organization that was founded in 1971 and won the Nobel Peace Prize in 1999. For years, MSF had to depend on commercial news organizations to cover its work, and had to hope that this coverage would reach and influence policymakers who could direct funding and other assistance to the areas where MSF was working. MSF was more adroit than many other relief organizations in attracting news coverage, but the news media have short attention spans and cannot be counted on. When news reports wane, lobbying and other forms of pressure have less chance of succeeding.

In recent years, however, MSF has developed an online presence that makes it an even more significant player in matters related to humanitarian assistance. Its websites (www.msf.org is the main one) constitute what is in effect the MSF news service, providing video and text reports about MSF projects around the world. The general public can turn to these sites, as well as to MSF's social media outlets, to learn what the organization is doing, and news media can use the sites' content as part of their own reporting. In 2014, the organization's US site, doctorswithoutborders.org, had more than five million visits. During the first half of 2015, Facebook likes totaled 918,000 and by the end of June 2015, Twitter followers had reached 486,000.[7] When an MSF hospital in Kunduz, Afghanistan was mistakenly attacked by US forces in 2015, MSF used its online presence to be certain that the world learned what had happened, providing video that was then used by some television news organizations.

This is an instance of new media serving as a political equalizer. Visibility increases political clout. MSF and other non-state actors can use new media to directly reach global publics and policymakers to a degree far beyond that which they could sustain in earlier years. With this increased visibility and control of information flow, the benign non-state actor has found a home among those advancing diplomatic interests.

Beyond using media, NGOs such as MSF must develop their

own diplomatic competence. When MSF sets up a field hospital in a war zone, MSF employees must negotiate with national and local governments as well as other parties to the conflict to ensure that the hospital's mission is respected.

Non-state players include major cities. In 1950, fewer than one billion people lived in cities. By 2050, 6.5 billion – which will then be two-thirds of all humanity – will be city dwellers. With the resultant concentrations of economic, political, and cultural influence, writes Ivo Daalder, cities "are no longer just places to live in. They have emerged as leading actors on the global stage."[8] Cities such as Sao Paulo and Shanghai have their own foreign affairs offices, coordinating with the cities' businesses, universities, and other institutions.

Given that cities are by far the world's largest consumers of energy and emitters of greenhouse gases, they must be recognized as significant participants in the diplomacy that addresses environmental concerns. Some cities have focused on a specific issue. In 1982, the mayor of Hiroshima, Japan, initiated Mayors for Peace, a group dedicated to having cities spread the word about the dangers of nuclear war. In 2003, the Association of Netherlands Municipalities helped counterparts in Rwanda to establish the Rwandese Association of Local Governments, which has worked to build effective and transparent local governments in that country.[9] In 2015, American and Chinese cities held their own summit to address their nations' climate change agendas. Two dozen of these cities devised their own timetables for climate-related reforms that were more ambitious than those of their national governments, and they explored ways to connect their clean-tech industries.[10]

Looking ahead, we are likely to see more cities networking

among themselves. In the Mega-Cities Project, representatives from 25 of the world's largest metropolitan areas share best practices. This project anticipates that by 2050, 3 billion people – almost a third of the world's population then – will be living in urban slums. It is logical that cities will increasingly engage in representing their own interests, rather than waiting for their national governments – with their own, more diverse agendas – to do so.[11]

In a diplomatic context, the role of cities poses some difficult questions. Should Japanese diplomats, for example, who are working on climate change as it relates to their region, deal with diplomats from China's foreign ministry or those from the city of Shanghai? In such instances, how much autonomous authority does the city have vis-à-vis the national government? That will vary from country to country (particularly as related to the legal authority behind cities' dealings), but the general point is that the world of diplomacy is growing more crowded.

International corporations are also non-state actors that possess immense influence but are adept at avoiding the scrutiny they deserve. Their interaction with diplomats is often indirect, but that does not mean that their power is diminished. In the global marketplace, everything from food to munitions is traded in ways that may be governed by treaties and other diplomatic agreements. Ripple effects, such as the impact on domestic jobs, keep political stakes high. Advances in communication and transportation, among other factors, mean that large-scale business is becoming almost uniformly international: Japanese cars assembled in the United States, American computers with Chinese microchips, and so on. Much of this is governed by the business community itself, but whenever diplomacy touches corporate operations, corporations assert themselves. As globalization accelerates, interaction between business and diplomacy will become more frequent and intense.

Immediately after the 2015 Iran nuclear agreement was signed, which called for lifting trade and other economic sanctions, Western corporations rushed to resuscitate previous business ties to Iran and create new ones. With a market of more than 80 million Iranians, commercial interests, as well as security matters, were not far in the background as the negotiations proceeded.

Corporations make their influence felt in ways beyond basic trade relationships. Google, with market capitalization estimated at US$370 billion as of early 2015, pursues a diplomatic agenda of its own, working with national governments in ways such as these:

- Meeting with an Israeli Knesset committee to discuss Google's decision to use "Palestine" rather than "Palestinian territories" on its products. Despite the Israeli government's objections, Google stayed with its decision.
- Google executives traveled to Cuba shortly before the resumption of Cuba–United States diplomatic relations to urge greater Internet freedom. The early trip was unsuccessful, but with formal ties restored, Google, along with US diplomats, can be expected to take the lead on this issue.
- During the 2014 Winter Olympics in Sochi, Russia, Google displayed a rainbow-colored image and an anti-discrimination quote from the Olympic Charter on its home page to implicitly criticize Russia's anti-gay policies.

As globalization becomes ever more the norm, multinational corporate giants such as Google, some of which have greater financial assets than many countries, will develop increasingly sophisticated "foreign policies" of their own. These companies will continue to be required to obey the laws of the countries in which they operate, but the degree to which they conform to – rather than dictate – evolving international norms on matters ranging from finance to environmental concerns to human rights will increasingly intrude on what used to be the uncontested domain of traditional diplomats.

Influence of non-state actors continues to grow. Because many of them skillfully use new media to reach larger publics, they are no longer isolated, and so they must be considered part of the mosaic of power that is the foundation of diplomacy. As the Atlantic Council reports, "it is no longer obvious who gets to participate in governance. In the Westphalian world, the answer was self-evident: the sovereign state and its designated representatives. In the Westphalian-Plus world, the answer is far from clear."[12]

In addition to incorporating non-state actors, diplomacy is extending into areas that are largely dependent on online capabilities. This is a virtual world, and it promises to add new dimensions to the practice of diplomacy.

## The virtual state

The virtual state exists *de facto*, not *de jure*. It reflects the growing obsolescence of traditional borders, represented by lines on maps and still usually respected by political institutions. One facet of the declining significance of traditional borders is the changing relevance of diasporic populations.

As an example, consider these questions: What is Pakistan? Is it simply the land mass northwest of India, or is it also the nine million Pakistanis who live overseas, with concentrations of over a million in the United Kingdom, Saudi Arabia, and the United Arab Emirates?[13] For diplomats, is Pakistan merely a traditional, physical entity, or is it a virtual state that encompasses much more than is reflected by maps and so must be addressed in innovative ways?

The big difference between members of a twenty-first-century diaspora and those of earlier times is the ability to retain, if they so choose, virtual connection with their homeland. During the surge of immigration from Europe to the United States during the late nineteenth and early twentieth centuries, immigrants saw advantages of assimilation in part because they were largely cut off from their homelands. Slow-moving letters were almost the only way to communicate. In today's new media era, the importance of distance diminishes as geography is superseded by technology.

Governments are recognizing that their diplomacy must address these well-connected diasporic populations. As part of its mission, CCTV directs its multilingual programming to overseas "Chinese" audiences, including those whose citizenship and primary language are no longer Chinese. Such international television content has long been available in some locales via satellite and cable systems, and now it is increasingly found on the internet, which means programmers need not worry about whether satellite proprietors or local carriers will accept their product. With news content in particular, to continue with CCTV as an example, the channel uses multiple platforms to deliver reports that are designed to appeal to a number of audiences, among them the Chinese diaspora and others interested in China. News programs subtly (and sometimes not so subtly) present China's political perspective on the world.

The Indian diaspora numbers 25 million, of whom nearly four

million (either born in India or reporting Indian ancestry or race) reside in the United States. One of the most significant roles for diasporic populations is to send remittances to their home countries. Indians lead the way in this, sending US$70 billion annually into the Indian economy. (India is followed by China at US$64 billion and the Philippines at US$28 billion.)[14] The Indian and US governments have collaborated to create the Indian Diaspora Investment Initiative (IDII), a mechanism to encourage the Indian diaspora to boost development in the home country. President Barack Obama and Prime Minister Narendra Modi invested their own political capital in this plan, which could be a prototype for other binational efforts to use diasporic resources in an organized way. International development analyst Deborah Trent notes that this is not an easy task: "Matching the US and Indian leaders' rhetoric of commitment to inclusive growth, monitoring of conditions, negotiation of interests, and evaluation of IDII results calls for participation of all stakeholder groups," which are numerous and are based in both the public and private sectors.[15]

Nations sometimes reach out to diasporas that are not their own. During relief efforts following the Haitian earthquake of 2010, the US government communicated with the Haitian diaspora within the United States – then more than 600,000 persons (and now more than 900,000) – as a principal way to connect with people within Haiti. The United States has also relied on the Somali diaspora in counterterrorism efforts directed at the Al Shabaab organization within Somalia. It should also be noted that the US government has been concerned with radicalization within the Somali diaspora in the United States.[16]

This underscores the need for balance in working with diasporas as part of the diplomatic enterprise. Intensive connectivity with the homeland can lead to questions about allegiances and can make assimilation seem less attractive to the newcomer, but it can also provide an additional diplomatic avenue into the home country.

No longer do new residents rely on postal services or find themselves disconnected not just from family and friends, but also from the politics and culture of their homeland. Instead, they can now remain virtually integrated within life back home. Whether by telephone, email, Facebook, or other modern media tool, connecting with the homeland has become standard practice for many in the diaspora. One study found that in 2002, 28 percent of immigrants called home at least once a week, and by 2009 the figure was 66 percent. Calls are decreasingly expensive, and seem an easy way to combat homesickness.[17]

The 2009 statistic above is based primarily on traditional phone services, but these are being overtaken by OTT ("Over-the-Top") telecoms that use the internet to make calls. Two of these, Viber and the Skype phone application, together have more than a billion users. Cheap and even free connectivity, as with other new media services, pulls the homeland closer, and stepping back into it does not require crossing any borders.

Physical distance is far less relevant, particularly as it relates to timeliness of communication. In her study of Arabic television viewing in Europe, Christina Slade wrote:

News from the country of origin is no longer, as it used to be, months old, nor is it mediated by others and shot through with nostalgic framing. Instead it is immediate, aired in the country of origin and the host country at the same time. Where once diasporic communities gathered and shared news of the country of birth in physical spaces such as cafes, they now can share the mediated public sphere of the heritage country in digital cyberspace.[18]

As with other aspects of the internet era, this reflects major changes in the notion of "community," with individuals (and their computers or mobile phones) relying less on face-to-face relationships and more on the virtual kind.

Government broadcasters have become fully cognizant of the diaspora-related diplomatic opportunities available in these cyber-venues. An example is the BBC World Service's BBC Persian Online, which attracts a smaller audience within Iran than in Iranian diasporic communities. Recognizing this, the BBC channel reports stories about the diaspora, as well as reporting about events in Iran, and this sometimes leads to a convergence of the audiences.[19]

This role amounts to more than simply disseminating information. One study of BBC Persian found that "as well as a channel of communication for diasporic consciousness and perspectives," Internet news sites can "mobilize and even construct diasporic communities."[20] This is a facet of the virtual state: a community of cultural and political interest that is provided a degree of structure by internet-based media.

On another level, this connectivity may alter the role of the diaspora in the economic and political life of the homeland. The ease of staying in touch and observing the homeland's civic life from afar can foster long-distance activism. In countries where news organizations are tightly controlled by the government, individual members of the diaspora, using telephone and social media, can provide a broader range of information than people in the homeland can access themselves.

If diplomatic strategy includes the ability to reach around conventional media to connect with targeted publics, diasporas provide an important route for doing so. More broadly, diasporas should be considered less as entities separate from the homeland and rather should be viewed as integral parts of virtual states.

The methods diasporas use to connect internally and externally may have diplomatic effect themselves. An example of this is Facebook.

## The Facebook factor

Is Facebook a gimmick, a useful tool, or something more? It certainly cannot be ignored. In little more than a decade, it has gone from a plaything for college students to an elemental facet of daily life for more than 1.5 billion people. On a personal level, Facebook has profoundly altered relationships among people. The occasional phone call or letter has been displaced by an almost constant flow of information. "Friends" let each other know what they are doing, sometimes with frequency and intimacy than ranges from fascinating to annoying.

Facebook's size and reach ensure global impact when it decides to take a stand on a policy matter. In June 2015, Facebook provided a free tool to allow its users to superimpose rainbow colors on their profile photos as a sign of endorsing gay marriage. Within three days, more than 26 million people did so, attracting more than 500 million "likes." The impact of such low-effort activism is debatable, but in subtle ways such gestures can influence the tone and substance of global discourse about an issue.[21]

Diplomats might be excused for dismissing Facebook as being

outside their realm of concerns. But then again . . . connections among more than a billion people must mean there are ways to put Facebook to work. The powers that be within Facebook recognize how influential they are. They speak of having their own foreign policy, which becomes manifest in their decisions about which countries they will work with. When in 2013 Facebook added Kosovo to its list of countries, it demonstrated its diplomatic clout. Although the United States and numerous other countries recognize Kosovo, the United Nations does not, largely because of Russia's protective stance toward Serbia. Many Kosovars did not want to be treated as de facto citizens of Serbia, and the Facebook decision helped them build their claim to an independent identity.

Diplomats see value in Facebook in that it gives them a means of communicating to a large audience without depending on the news media. One Facebook official cited the company's "foreign policy of the people," meaning a commitment to openness and "keeping Facebook up and running for people to use."

Despite its autonomy, Facebook must conform to national laws. In Turkey, for instance, it is illegal to make negative public statements about Kemal Ataturk, and so if such statements appear on Facebook and the Turkish government requests that they be removed, Facebook will comply. Facebook walks a narrow line in such matters. It tries to reconcile its commitment to openness with maintaining good relationships with governments, and it has leverage because it is an essential communication venue that governments want to use. That leverage becomes important when a politician is, for example, accused on Facebook of being corrupt and wants Facebook to pull down those comments. Since its birth, Facebook's stated purpose has been to "help people connect," and so an ethical question arises when it is asked to become a censor rather than a connecter. If the politician's request is not backed by law, Facebook will probably refuse to remove the material.

Facebook also holds immense amounts of personal information, and some governments believe that they, rather than this private corporation, should have oversight of that information. For its users in every country other than the United States, Facebook is an Irish corporation, and all non-US disputes related to protecting information are referred to the Irish Data Protection Authority. This saves Facebook from having to constantly deal with sometimes numerous regulatory bodies in each nation where it is present.

The equation of power comes down to this: by virtue of its vast constituency of easily accessed users, Facebook has become a player in modern diplomacy. Global discussion on Facebook has political impact, affecting policymakers who want to stay in step with opinions of those they represent and to influence others. Building diplomatic networks on Facebook is a relatively new concept, and although Facebook provides a logical forum for public diplomacy, the level of sophistication shown by many governments and interest groups remains low. Diplomats could learn valuable lessons from domestic political campaigns, such as those of Barack Obama in 2008 and 2012, which have shown that Facebook provides an effective means of identifying and pulling together people with shared interests.

Some countries, such as Israel, have recognized this and have proved themselves more skilled than others at using Facebook to mobilize supporters. Using Facebook to galvanize support within a far-flung diaspora is just one of the techniques that diplomats will find themselves needing to master during the coming years.

## Conflict and diplomacy

Diplomacy has long been a means of preventing and resolv-
ing conflict . . . or at least attempting to do so. It reached a new
level of importance during the Cold War, when the superpowers'
nuclear weapon stockpiles threatened the future of the planet. As
the possibility of war between the United States and the Soviet
Union receded, diplomats still found themselves interceding in
an endless array of conflicts large and small. In 2015, victims of
ongoing conflict – casualties and refugees – numbered well into
the millions.

So, does this mean diplomacy is ineffective in today's world
of conflict? The short answer is "No"; although war has not been
eradicated, diplomacy has saved countless lives by negotiating
cease-fires, pushing adversaries to resolve disputes, and champi-
oning humanitarian intervention. High-visibility diplomacy, such
as in the negotiations regarding Iran's nuclear capability, is still
valuable in forestalling potential conflict. Quieter diplomacy, such
as that between the United States and Cuba beginning in 2013,
helped reduce tensions within the Western hemisphere.

That is not to say that today's diplomacy will be fully adequate
in dealing with future conflicts. The same technological changes
that have affected so many other aspects of global affairs will
reshape conflict-related diplomacy.

First, diplomats will benefit from earlier warnings that might
prompt action to prevent mere problems from evolving into major
crises. In this way, diplomacy benefits from advances in intelligence gathering. When Russian-supported troops enter eastern
Ukraine, almost their every move can be tracked by using a combination of high-tech tools, ranging from mobile phone video

from people on the ground to sophisticated satellite imagery. When compared to the surveillance methods used during the 1962 Cuban missile crisis, such as U-2 reconnaissance flights, today's real-time capabilities can remove much guesswork from diplomatic maneuvers. This technology continues to advance, becoming more pervasive (some would say intrusive) and more effective at undermining efforts at deception. Diplomacy receives a boost when knowledge replaces speculation.

More complicated is the expansion of conflict into the cyber-world. Hacking and denial-of-service attacks have so far been harmful annoyances, but not acts of war. Some countries, however, are nearing the point of technological capabilities at which they could launch electronic attacks that shut down financial markets, emergency services, transportation systems, and other essential aspects of national life. A nation so attacked could consider a state of war to exist with the attacker (assuming it could be identified) and respond in kind or with traditional weaponry.

In a world in which so many institutions and individuals are dependent on new technologies, an electronic *casus belli* is not far-fetched, and so a whole new array of preventive stratagems must become part of the diplomatic repertoire. Diplomats need not become full-fledged techies, but foreign ministries are likely to recruit more technology professionals to provide the expertise required to navigate this field. Treaties and other agreements to prevent cyber misbehavior will need to reflect up-to-date complexities of evolving technology.

Non-state actors can be expected to wield disproportionate power in such matters. You don't need tanks if you have geeks. As with conventional terrorism, a small group of motivated and skilled adversaries could cause havoc that might confound diplomatic and military strategists.

On this topic, pertinent lessons can be found from conflicts of about 2,500 years ago, when Scythians mastered the art of asymmetric warfare: fighting their enemy on their own terms, not the enemy's. Robert Kaplan noted that as today's insurgents in various places adopt the Scythians' tactics of skirmish and harass (with guns or computers), the United States and other major powers have realized that they have "only limited ability to determine the outcome of many conflicts, despite being a superpower. America is learning an ironic truth of empire: you endure by *not* fighting every battle." Kaplan asked, "If the U.S. helps topple the dictator Bashar al-Assad on Wednesday, then what will it do on Thursday, when it finds it has helped midwife to power a Sunni jihadist regime, or on Friday, when ethnic cleansing of the Shia-trending Alawites commences?" Kaplan advises that the United States "remain a half-step removed – caution, after all, is not the same as capitulation."[22] Friends and enemies are more difficult to identify.

With lessons from the past and prognostication about the likely future, diplomats are continuing to adjust to a world in which warfare is changing in many ways. During the early years of the Cold War, the most likely major war would have involved conventional forces once again tearing up Europe. Soon after, preventing nuclear war became a principal object of diplomacy. The Vietnam War signaled a shift toward the Scythian model, which appeared again in Afghanistan, Iraq, and elsewhere. If diplomats are to prevent or conclude conflict in its many pervasive forms, they must understand military history, strategy, and tactics. War is too important to be left to the generals.

## Religion and diplomacy

Religious studies scholar Huston Smith observed, "The surest way to the heart of a people is through their faith."[23] That would seem to place religion at the center of diplomatic strategy, particularly regarding public diplomacy, but religion's role in diplomacy varies greatly around the world. For some countries it is a central part of foreign policy, and in others it is circled warily. Its broad effect on culture and on public opinion is often little understood. Barry Rubin noted, "In modern times, religion has increasingly been seen in the West as a theological set of issues rather than a profoundly political influence in public life."[24] Depending on the nature of the state and the culture, separation between the theological and the political may be a fundamental premise, or this division may not exist at all.

In Islamic countries, depending on the balance between theocratic and state-based influences, diplomacy is presumed to be infused with religion in the same way that other governmental practices are. But when diplomats from countries such as Iran sit down with those from the West to discuss nuclear policy and other matters, traditional strategic interests as well as precepts of Islam drive the negotiations.

Iran's principal rival for regional influence, Sunni-dominated Saudi Arabia, also emphasizes religion in its diplomacy, often in the form of moves to counter Iranian or other Shi'a-related initiatives. WikiLeaks documents, according to the *New York Times*, "illustrate a near obsession with Iran" on the part of the Saudis, and provide evidence of Saudi "government agencies plotting moves to limit the spread of Shiite Islam." Saudi diplomacy extends to missionary activity, and includes "putting foreign preachers on the Saudi payroll, building mosques, schools and study centers, and undermining foreign officials and news media deemed threatening to the kingdom's agenda." In one of the documents, from 2011, the Saudi foreign minister requested aid for flood victims in Thailand, noting that "it will have a positive effect on Muslims in Thailand and will restrict the Iranian government in expanding its Shiite influence."[25]

Roman Catholic leaders have also overtly employed religious diplomacy. Dispatching papal envoys dates back to the earliest days of the Church, but two recent popes, John Paul II and Francis, have conducted religion-based diplomacy with an intensity and effect that has made the Vatican a more significant force in global affairs. By addressing topics such as the evils of communism and the dangers of climate change, and by taking advantage of global media exposure, they have modernized Vatican diplomacy and expanded the breadth of the influence of the Catholic Church on certain issues.

Pope Francis has enthusiastically embraced social media. He has nearly seven million followers on Twitter, and uses that medium's brief messages to address his favorite issues, such as global warming. An example: "A great challenge: stop ruining the garden which God has entrusted to us so that all may enjoy it."[26]

Most Western governments have embraced secularism in much of their diplomacy. American diplomats have almost always treated religion delicately, made wary of religion in public affairs by the American principle of separating church and state. That principle's relevance to foreign, as opposed to domestic, policy-making is questionable, and US presidents have never been shy about invoking God whenever convenient, but secularism continues to be integral to US diplomacy. Secretary of State Madeleine

Albright observed that many practitioners of foreign policy "have sought to separate religion from world politics, to liberate logic from beliefs that transcend logic."[27]

Albright, however, also noted "the immense power of religion to influence how people, think, feel, and act." She wrote: "Religion at its best can reinforce the core values necessary for people from different cultures to live in some degree of harmony; we should make the most of that possibility."[28]

Albright wrote that passage several years after terrorist attacks had raised tensions between the Muslim and non-Muslim worlds. Those tensions continue and have been exacerbated by the rise of the Islamic State, which wrapped its Middle East conquests in religious trappings. Even if a case for secularist diplomacy could have been made in the past, the present and future will demand greater integration of religious matters within diplomatic strategies. The US State Department has created new positions to reach out to religious leaders and communities (especially Muslim), and some officials endorse adding a religion attaché to every embassy's staff.

Activist popes and increased focus on Islam are among the factors making religion more central in diplomacy, and even countries that are committed to political secularism at home need to recognize that their diplomacy must reflect this reality.

The importance of religion to the future of diplomacy is another example of the changes brought about by the rise of new media. Beginning with religious programming carried by satellite television and radio channels, and continuing with heavy messaging on social media, religious communication has reached unprecedented levels of volume and reach. When someone such as controversial Egyptian theologian Yusuf al-Qaradawi appears on Al Jazeera and follows up his televised commentary with postings on Facebook, which might quickly pick up a quarter-million "likes," and on Twitter, where he has more than a million followers, he is undoubtedly having an impact, and diplomats watching the Arab world should pay attention. They should also pay attention to those who champion viewpoints different than those Qaradawi espouses and can reach their own large cyber-audiences.

Some states are inseparable from their religious identity, while for many others, religion's relationship to their diplomacy is more amorphous. The world as a whole is becoming less secular, and although Christianity and Islam together constitute a majority (55 percent) among the world's population, smaller religions can prove significant in diplomatic matters. Judaism, for example, has only about 14 million adherents – 0.2 percent of the world's population – and 11 million of them live in either Israel or the United States. And yet Judaism's history and the current political prominence of Israel would seem to make knowledge about this religion a necessity for diplomats.

To return to a far larger religion, it is hard to believe that some diplomats posted to predominantly Muslim countries have never read the Qur'an or been instructed in the often nuanced meanings of this foundation of Islam. Such reluctance to include learning about relevant religions in diplomatic training and practice should be consigned to the past. The diplomacy of the future must accord religion its appropriate place in global relationships.

The issues discussed in this chapter pull diplomacy into meeting broader responsibilities and challenges. The neatness of the Westphalian order has become a more crowded and faster-moving environment. States and non-states have proliferated since the days when an era's superpowers commanded most of diplomats' attention. Now, the doors of the club have been thrown open to newly influential real and virtual actors. Diplomats need to know more and do more.

That said, there should be limits to diplomacy's responsibilities, and the next chapter examines the interference and detours about which diplomats must be aware.

# 4

# Staying on Track

Diplomats have become accustomed to the distractions of domestic politics and the machinations of bureaucracies. They find themselves being pulled this way and that, with their diplomatic skills being tested not just in dealings with other nations but also finding their way through the partisan and governmental mazes of their own country. Although being based at the State Department or foreign ministry keeps diplomats near the center of power, those who are assigned to distant posts may welcome their status as outliers in political battles. To a limited extent, they can go about their business without being sucked into the political whirlpool.

Avoiding traps laid by a hostile legislator or fending off intrusion by another government agency can consume much time and psychic energy. Rivalries flourish and the insularity diplomats might wish for has become harder to secure due to tighter reins of accountability, or just plain meddling. Keeping focused on diplomatic tasks and goals requires a mix of self-discipline and political acumen.

# Perils of politics

Once upon a time, diplomats lived within a fortress from which the evils of partisanship were usually excluded. The diplomats could go about their business with all due dignity. They had much in common in terms of education, family background, and self-regard. They spoke only to one another (preferably in French) and let no lesser mortals intrude upon their stewardship of relations among states. As Michael Binyon observed, diplomats learned "the art of negotiation and the trademark suavity that concealed a Machiavellian mind."[1] Occasionally they took note of domestic political maneuvering, just to reassure themselves that such matters were beneath them. When they found themselves compelled to plunge into the political swamp, they usually did so reluctantly.

Today, such distancing is truly a fairy tale. However clubby diplomats became and however removed from grubby partisanship they liked to imagine themselves, they have never been fully divorced from the realities of politics, and today they are more scrutinized and subject to political pressures than ever before. Budgets, approval of appointments, interagency squabbling, and the like are inescapable.

To an extent, that political engagement is as it should be. Diplomatic history is replete with instances of misjudgments and well-meaning efforts that have gone astray, due, at least in part, to insufficient accountability. Oversight is essential. In the United States and many parliamentary democracies, diplomats are among those whom legislative bodies call upon to explain their nation's international relationships, and to evaluate threats and opportunities. This is linkage to the public, and in theory the legislative and executive branches of government should be able to air their differences and then proceed in a spirit of reasonable accord.

That may be yet another fairy tale. In reality, diplomacy and politics are inextricably linked in an often contentious relationship, and political concerns can reach a point at which diplomatic quality and integrity are undermined.

Politicization of diplomacy takes place in a number of ways. A persistent controversy in the United States concerns the de facto selling of ambassadorships – nominating women and men who have made substantial campaign contributions to the incumbent president or other elected officials. Every president does this, some more overtly than others. Richard Nixon, in grand jury testimony after he had resigned from the presidency, defended the appointment of ambassadors who had contributed large amounts to his campaigns. Further, so he might reap domestic political gain, "I asked for at least two Italians [and] one or two who might be of Polish background." Justifying his ambassadorial criteria, Nixon added, "As far as career ambassadors, most of them are a bunch of eunuchs . . . in an emotional sense, in a mental sense."[2]

Nixon was odd; that is well established. But in this practice, he was far from unique. As of December 2014, of President Barack Obama's ambassadorial appointments, 35 percent were political rather than career diplomats. By comparison, Obama's two most recent predecessors, George W. Bush and Bill Clinton, had selected 29 and 28 percent political appointees, respectively.

Sometimes the political nominees have valuable non-diplomatic experience, such as academic expertise about the country where they serve or business acumen that proves useful in fostering trade relationships. Nominees might have symbolic value, as when Caroline Kennedy was named ambassador to

Japan. And occasionally the cost of maintaining ambassadorial residences and social obligations far exceed ambassadors' salaries, so wealthy women and men are selected for those posts. But numerous other political selections have been based solely on campaign support and some of these people have been embarrassingly unqualified. This degrades diplomatic service generally.

The US Senate is responsible for confirming ambassadorial appointments, and occasionally the ineptitude of the nominees becomes obvious during the confirmation hearings and is captured for the world to watch on newscasts and YouTube.[3] But the Senate rarely rejects anyone because Democrats and Republicans play the same game, rewarding friends and supporters with ambassadorships. Occasionally, and usually for partisan reasons, a temporary "hold" is placed on the nomination of an ambassador, regardless of her or his qualifications. This can leave the ambassadorial post vacant for some time, which may damage relations with the host country.

Among major powers, the United States is the only one to so overtly politicize the ambassadorial appointment process. Correcting this situation should not be difficult; legislation to ensure a more professional corps of ambassadors exists but is regularly ignored. The Foreign Service Act of 1980 sets out, among other provisions, the requirement that nominees "possess clearly demonstrated competence" to do the job, including knowledge of the history, culture, institutions, and language of the country to which she or he will be sent. The act also states, "Contributions to political campaigns should not be a factor in the appointment."[4]

Although current practice is wrong and a statutory remedy exists, there is no indication that this latter-day spoils system is going to change. The quality of US diplomacy is damaged, and other countries look on, amused and horrified (although they, too, have their foibles).

This situation illustrates the dangers of partisanship encroaching on diplomatic standards. The principle that "politics stops at the water's edge" has never been fully realized, except perhaps briefly in wartime, and in democracies today foreign policy is seen as fair game for those who hunt political trophies.

The topic often attracting the sharpest political attention is trade. Elected officials are always sensitive about potential threats to their constituents' jobs. Because of this, commercial diplomacy (boosting economic activity) and economic diplomacy (achieving political objectives) must move along a narrow path, not straying into minefields laid by diverse parties. Some business interests will want help in accessing foreign markets, while others favor protection from foreign competition. Labor unions have similar concerns. This process is difficult enough when only two countries are involved, and complexity grows exponentially when multiple states are negotiating.

Diplomats are not usually in a position to push back against domestic political pressure, especially when that pressure is amplified by well-organized interest groups. Whether a labor union or an ethnic organization, many such groups have mastered the art of rousing the public about diplomatic issues that hit closer to home than most people first realize. Using social media expertly, special interests are adept at mobilizing their core constituencies and making their case to larger publics.

In the United States, the most effective special interest related to foreign policy is the amalgam of groups that support Israel. Any time that issues related to Israel's relationships with its neighbors are the subjects of policy debate, backers of Israel mobilize and apply pressure on Congress, the White House, the State Department, the news media, and other centers of influence. As with ambassadorships, campaign contributions play a significant role in this, ensuring that contributors' arguments are heard. A case can be made that the pro-Israel political forces are efficient in their advocacy and therefore their frequent success is evidence that the democratic process works. Others might see this as the triumph of politics over the true foreign policy interests of the United States.

Sometimes an interest group does not have quite enough political (or financial) muscle to change policy. Each year, the Armenian-American community urges Congress to designate as genocide the slaughter of Armenians by Turkey during and soon after the First World War. Turkey strongly objects to this proposed measure, and as a member of NATO with great geopolitical importance, its diplomats can complain to the White House and produce enough pushback to undermine the Armenian-Americans' efforts in Congress.

Such lobbying efforts may continue for decades before finally losing their effectiveness. That was the case with the Cuban-American groups that for a half-century lobbied successfully against renewed ties between the United States and Cuba. Finally, the Obama administration made the diplomatic and political judgment that recognition should be restored.

The news media could play a larger role in foreign policy debates, providing forums for the objective viewpoints that interest groups eschew and offering coverage that offsets one-sided arguments. But news organizations may find themselves outmaneuvered by those who understand journalism better than journalists understand politics. During the run-up to the 2003 US invasion of Iraq, most American news media were consistently "handled" by the George W. Bush administration and failed to ask tough questions about the reasons for going to war. Put simply, the news media failed, and as a result debate about a crucial issue was inadequate.

This was also a case in which at least a modicum of partisanship would have been helpful to generate substantive debate before going to war. Along with the news media, the opposition Democratic Party was extraordinarily inept in contesting the Bush administration's inflated claims about the necessity of regime change in Iraq.

So, this is the conundrum. Partisanship can impair effective diplomacy, but it can also provide essential democratic balance to the mandate under which diplomats work.

Looking ahead, new media tools will foster more intense partisan involvement in foreign policy. Facebook groups and the like can be rallied in a few moments, and political parties can easily identify interest subgroups within their constituencies. As with so many aspects of public life, the speed and reach of this kind of political pressure will grow, and so even when senior policymakers try to shield their representatives in the field from this, diplomats are likely to feel the heat of partisanship as they go about their work.

## Diplomacy diffused: who's in charge?

For this part of the chapter, the governmental solar system of the United States will be the basis for considering two questions: where *should* diplomacy reside, and where *does* it reside?

In the US executive branch, the sun around which all else revolves is the White House. Some autonomy exists for the individual cabinet branches and other agencies, but only in so far as the White House allows it to exist. President Harry Truman noted that "The buck stops here," and the corollary to that is, "Power starts here."

The Senate must ratify treaties, Congress as a whole must decide on funding for overseas programs, and the federal courts may play a role if Constitutional questions arise, but in terms of setting the nation's international course, the ultimate arbiter of foreign policy and diplomatic endeavors is the president, although many presidencies have been marred by the chief executive's indecision, reversing course, and other problematic diplomatic behavior. The White House has a foreign policy bureaucracy of its own, at the heart of which is the National Security Council (NSC). During the Obama administration, the NSC had a staff of 370 people, more than ten times the size of the staff when Henry Kissinger headed this office in the 1970s.[5] It had not become ten times more efficient.

For a time, Kissinger served as both National Security Adviser and Secretary of State, although he always paid most attention to his White House role. Given how thoroughly Kissinger had usurped the authority of his predecessor at the State Department, William Rogers, the de facto merger of offices had little practical effect. President Gerald Ford, after living with this arrangement for a while, limited Kissinger to the State Department only and picked a new National Security Adviser, Brent Scowcroft.

This bit of history is important because it illustrates the lack of clarity concerning assignment of responsibilities. Regardless of who is president, State Department officials regularly complain that they have been "big-footed" by the NSC or others at the White House. A secretary of state with an independent political power base, such as Hillary Rodham Clinton, may have more leeway than others, but even during her tenure at State, some of the subcabinet appointees within the State Department – such as under secretaries and assistant secretaries – were selected by the White House.

This situation is not lost on diplomats in the field or on policymakers of other countries. It is a significant issue because if you are perceived as not having real authority, why should anyone spend time working with you? Again, if you have the star power of Clinton, the problem is mitigated somewhat, but real power is known to exist in one place.

Compounding this problem is the general dispersion of foreign policy responsibilities. The Department of Defense might be presumed to be content with its own important duties, but it sometimes strays onto the turf of others. Because so many countries rely on military assistance from the United States, generals may have more clout than ambassadors. Further, given its large budget, the Pentagon is inclined to wander into areas that might be thought to be outside its purview. Public diplomacy? The Pentagon has mounted its own efforts at "strategic communication," more recently known as "Strategic Engagement and Communication,"[6] that mirror some State Department programs. When Robert Gates was Secretary of Defense, he recognized the imbalance in resources and overlap in functions. He advocated giving some of the Defense Department's money to the State Department. That will happen only rarely.

Of course, in a globalized society, every cabinet agency will have some diplomatic duties: the Treasury Department with international monetary matters; the Commerce Department with trade issues; the Justice Department, with international legal issues; and so on. Determining who has responsibility for what can be a complex task in itself, and Washington is filled with lawyers and lobbyists who, for substantial fees, will help their clients navigate the maze.

When areas of responsibility are in question and turf wars break out, the White House acts as referee (unless legislation mandates a specific Congressional role or particular court rulings are applicable). Interagency relationships are predictably complex, but just within fundamental tasks of diplomacy, the existence of mini-empires can cause difficulties.

During the Kennedy administration, numerous foreign economic assistance programs were brought together as the United States Agency for International Development (USAID). With funding approved by Congress, USAID operates as an independent federal agency, working along lines of foreign policy priorities set by the president, the secretary of state, and the NSC.

Given the resources it dispenses, USAID is one of the most visible facets of US foreign policy. It directly assists foreign publics and is therefore at the heart of America's public diplomacy mission. Looking ahead, and assuming that public diplomacy should play a more central role in overall foreign relations, it might be worth considering bringing aid programs into the State Department proper and making USAID part of the domain of the Under Secretary for Public Diplomacy and Public Affairs (and at the same time spinning off the public affairs element into a free-standing office of its own).

This would not be an arcane bureaucratic maneuver. This kind of restructuring is fundamental to designing the future of diplomacy. Aid programs, if they are creative and thoughtfully targeted, have immeasurable value in international relations. Beyond political considerations, they also have humanistic value. One US program, the President's Emergency Plan for AIDS Relief (PEPFAR), created during the George W. Bush administration and renewed and expanded during the Obama presidency, illustrates this impact. Directed primarily to southern Africa, PEPFAR, as of September 2014, was supporting antiretroviral treatment for nearly 8 million persons, HIV testing and counseling for more than 14 million pregnant women, and care for more than 5 million orphans and vulnerable children.[7]

PEPFAR's work is implemented by seven US government agencies: the Departments of State, Defense, Labor, Commerce, and Health and Human Services; USAID; and the Peace Corps. That interagency structure is inherently cumbersome, and at some point a president or secretary of state might find ways to streamline this and similar programs.

PEPFAR is the kind of program that might not generate much domestic publicity or political gain, but as an instrument of public diplomacy it can win more than transient popular favor in the countries where it operates.

Every major and aspiring power dispenses aid of one kind or another. Cynics might argue that these programs are designed solely to buy popularity, but the recipients of assistance are unlikely to care about motives. They are likely to view favorably the country that provided aid that saved a child's life. That, too, is part of diplomacy.

Whether in the United States or elsewhere, the organization of diplomacy in many instances creaks with old age. Priorities become obsolete, battles over jurisdiction are fought, efforts are duplicated, money is wasted . . . the list goes on. The results of this atrophied process should cause dismay, but too many policymakers have become so accustomed to and comfortable with the status quo that meaningful reforms are rare. Even when the desire to change the system exists, the prospect of a nasty political fight with entrenched interests may discourage all but the most resolute reformers.

## Mission creep

A government bureaucracy is a predictable beast. When it catches the scent of money, it moves in that direction, no matter how far from home. Sometimes this pursuit takes it into domains unsuitable for operational success, but if funding is to be found, it plunges ahead.

Such has been the case when American diplomats have tried their hand at fighting terrorism. In Washington, just say "counterterrorism" and money will float down from heaven (or from Congress), without much concern about the appropriateness of the recipient. At the State Department, the public diplomacy division received such a windfall to counter the online messaging of the Islamic State through the Center for Strategic Counterterrorism Communication.

The IS online videos are filled with lies. They rely on a blasphemous interpretation of Islam to lure young fighters into combat against fellow Muslims, and they promise a quick trip to paradise for "martyrs" who throw away their lives. To an outsider, the flimsiness of the IS case is apparent, but the online recruiting has been done skillfully, relying on carefully considered psychological insight and preying on disaffected young men and women who yearn for the meaningful lives that the IS offers them.

Meanwhile, the State Department toils mightily to produce a counter-argument. Their online products, such as "Think Again, Turn Away" messages, have stressed the murderous nature of IS and focused on its victims. But the State Department is required by law to take ownership of its work. Consider the effect on credibility of the US messaging if even the most forceful anti-IS video concludes with the State Department seal appearing on screen.

Much more effective would be a bare-knuckles operation: no disclaimers and a product that matched up better against the videos coming from Al Hayat, the IS video production arm (the name, meaning "Life," was stolen from the pan-Arab newspaper, *Al-Hayat*). The proper US home for such an effort would be the intelligence agencies. No requirement for official disclaimers there; the agency could put a logo similar to Al Hayat's in the corner of the screen and mimic the stirring martial tone of the IS material, but make the content as forcefully anti-IS as possible. Then push it out into the swift current of YouTube, Twitter, and other online venues. It would find its audience.

Just the fact that the State Department has undertaken this kind of task underscores the broadened – and perhaps opportunistic – definition of "diplomacy." Growing emphasis on public diplomacy opens the door to being assigned tasks such as counterterrorism, but assuming that people trained as diplomats are skilled in this field is illogical. Dealing with terrorist organizations, even just at the level of discouraging recruitment, is not diplomacy; it is a street fight.

If diplomacy is to be effective in the future, it must design and adapt to new structural, as well as technological, realities. There has never been a bureaucracy that would not benefit from being reduced in size and from having lines of authority drawn more clearly. At the same time, diplomacy must not become overextended. Possibilities for expanding into tangential fields may be alluring, but they are best resisted.

## What should diplomats know?

Diplomats' training remains relatively conventional, and in many countries haphazard. In the United Kingdom, for example, it was just in 2015 that the Foreign and Commonwealth Office launched its Diplomatic Academy, which featured a skeletal curriculum of basic topics. When the Diplomatic Academy opened, Christopher Meyer, who had served as British ambassador to the United States, observed, "Over centuries the qualities that make a good diplomat have not changed: you must be able to negotiate, to build networks of influence, to have a profound understanding of a foreign society, and to acquire information for rapid, accurate reporting to London – and all in the service of the national interest." He also noted that these skills had been in decline for several reasons: "the undue importance given to multilateral diplomacy (i.e., conferences on transnational issues) at the expense of bilateral diplomacy between states; an obsession with managerialism and the alchemy of outside consultants; and the deployment of significant but scarce resources to consular activity, to rescue tourists in distress."[8]

Not all diplomats will agree with Meyer's assessment, but his comments reflect the challenges of modernizing a profession steeped in tradition. The creation of the Diplomatic Academy, like the US Foreign Service Institute (which was born in 1947), recognizes that merely holding an Oxbridge (or Ivy League) degree is no longer sufficient for a career in diplomacy. Like law or medicine, diplomacy requires specialized preparation – solid academic instruction and then on-the-job professional training. The Foreign Service Institute (FSI) has a large campus just outside Washington, DC and offers more than 600 courses – ranging in length from one day to two years, including training in 70 languages – to more than 100,000 enrollees each year from the State Department and numerous other agencies and the military.[9]

Whether a small start-up, such as the Diplomatic Academy, or a huge operation such as FSI, the challenge for administrators is to ensure the appropriate breadth of training. For diplomats going to the Middle East, for instance, knowledge of the Qur'an is essential to understanding the cultural milieu within which they will be working. If going to Russia, an appreciation of what the Soviet Union endured during the Second World War is necessary to comprehend the motivation behind contemporary Russian foreign policy. And so forth. The key to all this is that training must be outward-looking and address the political and cultural realities with which diplomats in their postings will contend.

In addition, diplomatic training must include fundamental technological skills and the rules that govern their use. Given how quickly this field changes, with updated and new tech devices appearing regularly, training must keep pace. The most effective way to do this, and to refresh knowledge across a wide range of topics, is to rely heavily on what used to be known as "distance learning." Using online platforms is cost-effective and is the logical way to keep diplomats current. Some countries bring their heads of missions home once a year, but these sessions are mainly to discuss policy. The online teaching venues that universities and corporations use are interactive and suitable for training in everything from languages to crisis management, and content can be easily updated as needed.

Recruitment could also be reformed. The United States relies on a merit-based examination system, but might add flexibility to enlist more people with special talents – language, knowledge about a particular region, tech skills – to mix with the generalists.

The role of the embassy itself should also be reviewed in light of political and technological changes. Because of security concerns, some countries, including the United States, have turned their embassies into fortresses and relocated them to suburbs or other places where public access can be tightly controlled. Further, in certain high-risk locations, diplomats' movements are strictly limited. They rarely leave the embassy premises, and when they do, they may be accompanied by fierce-looking bodyguards.

Given the number of attacks on embassies and consulates by terrorist organizations and others, these moves make sense in terms of basic security judgment. Diplomats are not supposed to be combatants, but this distancing has a price beyond construction costs. Particularly in a time when public diplomacy is of growing importance, barriers between diplomats and publics are disruptive. A balance must be struck; tipping too far toward being "secure" impairs the quality of diplomats' work.

The "virtual embassy" is not a substitute except in special circumstances. The United States has virtual embassies for Iran, where the embassy building was seized during the 1979 revolution, and Syria, where political and security realities make on-site embassy operations impossible. These embassies' websites are much like those of physical embassies, and they at least ensure a form of continuing presence. There are, however, no American diplomats in Tehran or Damascus who directly interact with the countries' citizens.

Virtual embassies and the more common "fortress" embassies appeal to some policymakers because so much of the embassies' work can apparently be done within the secure confines of the internet. As was noted in chapter 2 regarding using virtual representation in public diplomacy, the decision to replace real with virtual should not be taken lightly. Human diplomats still have value.

The importance of diplomats directly interacting with foreign constituencies is underscored by the concept of the "expeditionary diplomat." As articulated by former US Under Secretary of State Marc Grossman and others, this idea runs counter to the tide of tech reliance and is based on the notion that diplomats should be more visible and activist. The roots of this are found in the work carried out in post-conflict reconstruction and stabilization projects, and supplemental specialized training would be provided by the military and other sources outside the domain of usual diplomatic preparation.

This is another facet of public diplomacy and another step away from traditionally heavy reliance on the diplomat-to-diplomat duties that for so long constituted most of a diplomat's workload. In some postings, this role would also mean addressing concerns related to diplomats' personal safety. This latter issue is important, because in some countries diplomats are targets and the "expeditionary" approach may carry with it an increased level of risk. But risks must be balanced against the potential gains accrued by having closer contacts with the communities in which the diplomats are serving.

If diplomats are doing their expeditionary work well, word will spread. A YouTube video or a Facebook posting showing diplomats working with the public can be helpful in shaping opinion. Social media are becoming more localized, as well as more global, in their reach. Neighborhood media networks are taking hold in some countries. Their content is often about residents seeking a competent plumber or searching for a lost pet, but they also would be effective in convening people to meet with a diplomat to discuss the character and needs of the particular community. Obviously, there are limits related to scale; diplomatic field presence depends on the availability of personnel and other factors. But public diplomacy's effectiveness is incremental, and every small effort contributes to the larger picture.

The art of diplomacy cannot be static. To be effective, it must evolve to meet new needs and respond to new opportunities. As with many of the other issues discussed in this book, media-related capabilities are integral to defining the scope of diplomatic duties. When media's reach and versatility expand, so too do the possibilities for diplomatic achievements increase. The next chapter examines the breadth of diplomacy's prospects as the future of diplomacy takes shape.

# 5

# Shaping Diplomacy's Future

In July 2015, when the agreement concerning Iran's nuclear program was reached, the public learned about it not just from formal
announcements passed through the filter of news organizations,
but directly from the negotiators themselves. Foreign ministries
used social media to deliver the information in first-person fashion, and then the public jumped in.

Federica Mogherini, Minister for Foreign Affairs of the
European Union, tweeted: "Talks done. We have the agreement."
Soon thereafter, US Secretary of State John Kerry tweeted, "P5+1
plus #Iran reached agreement, bringing insight & accountability
to nuclear program – not for small # of yrs, but lifetime of program." As this news spread, an online map of Iran, courtesy of the
BBC, lit up as it showed concentrations of Iranian tweets about the
agreement emanating from Tehran and elsewhere.

At 7 a.m. in Washington, DC, President Barack Obama held a
news conference about the deal, choosing the odd time in order
to reach audiences in time zones other than his own. Iranian

President Hassan Rouhani used Twitter to urge his English-language followers to tune in to Iran's TV coverage. Israeli Prime Minister Benjamin Netanyahu linked his Twitter feed to video of his statement: "The world is a much more dangerous place today than it was yesterday." Netanyahu's Twitter feed, @IsraeliPM, then featured quotes from his statement in individual tweets. Meanwhile, the White House was using Twitter, @WhiteHouse, to frame the agreement from the Obama administration's perspective, using graphics that advanced the administration's position.

President Rouhani's tweets from @HassanRouhani made the case that the agreement was in Iran's best interest. In Washington, once Obama's news conference concluded, 15 principal US government Twitter feeds, ranging from Vice President Joseph Biden's to that of the US Embassy in Tel Aviv, pushed out the administration's case. Similarly, the US State Department put its many social media sites to work: Facebook, Google+, Flickr, YouTube, and its DipNote blog. The European Union and others also provided links to the agreement itself, the Joint Comprehensive Plan of Action.[1]

Hammering out the agreement had been an exercise in traditional negotiation, with all the complexities and tensions that process entails. But then the new diplomacy took center stage. As is noted elsewhere in this book, these social media reports were merely a prelude to a fierce debate about the merits of the agreement, much of which took place on the internet. The announcement itself is important because it underscored themes we encounter consistently as we move into diplomacy's future: speed; direct contact with and involvement of the public; breadth of the audience for such messaging; diplomats' anticipation of swift reaction from the public at large and from special interest constituencies.

As the future of diplomacy takes shape, such matters will help define the missions and competencies of diplomats.

## Two-tier diplomacy

Traditional diplomacy is alive and well. It will remain healthy, but it will share the stage with a newer, more public-oriented diplomacy. It will be up to practitioners across the board not just to ensure peaceful coexistence between old and new, but also to take full advantage of their complementary strengths.

Even the traditional aspects of diplomacy are changing. For one thing, the profession is no longer an all-male preserve. Women are increasingly wielding influence as heads of government, foreign ministers, leaders of international organizations, and in private sector jobs that affect international economics and politics.

Also, the dispersion of global power among a growing number of states, as opposed to the two-superpower dominance during the Cold War, adds complexity to diplomatic calculations. This spreading of influence means that although basic nation-to-nation diplomacy remains essential, setting priorities is a more complicated task. During the Cold War, US–Soviet dealings and collisions took place on Olympus, while mere mortals watched and braced for aftershocks. The American opening to China in 1972 foreshadowed the leveling of Olympus, or at least its reduction from mountain to hill. During the decades since then, many more states and non-states have become important players.

Amidst all this geopolitical reshuffling, one constant is the importance of personalities. Lawrence Wright's *Thirteen Days in September*, which brings a microscopic focus to the 1978 Camp

David negotiations between Jimmy Carter, Anwar Sadat, and Menachem Begin, describes how prospects for the Middle East were affected as much by the people involved as by the issues they addressed. As Wright observed, "There is never a perfect time or ideal people to bring an end to bloody conflicts, and unlike the talent for war, the ability to make peace has always been rare."[2] The abilities, ideals, and idiosyncrasies of the three men were diplomatic issues in themselves because they were so significant in shaping the course of the negotiations.

Today, personalities remain inextricably linked to the workings of diplomacy. Barack Obama, Angela Merkel, Xi Jinping, Michelle Bachelet, Paul Kagame, Vladimir Putin; each has his or her own attitudes and style that affect aspects of their foreign policies and how they work with their counterparts around the world. They are not diplomats in the conventional sense, but they determine the policies that guide diplomats' work. Regardless of the technological influences on diplomacy, we should never lose sight of the importance of the *people* who shape the substance of international affairs.

The psychology of diplomacy will remain important, and in the future will affect not just traditional face-to-face dealings, but also will be seen in the ways that new technological tools are put to use. World leaders will be certain that their inner circles include nerds who are adept at using these tools. The leaders' personal attitudes about the value of technology will help determine the balance between traditional and new diplomatic technique.

Aside from the conventional array of heads of government and foreign ministers, new participants will be taking seats at the virtual diplomatic table. Non-state actors will continue to avail themselves of the increased visibility and resulting political clout that new media allow, and so they will demand that more attention be paid to their interests. In the past many groups on the fringes of the international community could be ignored, or at least dealt with peremptorily, because it was difficult for them to build a constituency. As the case of the Islamic State illustrates, an outsider today can use media to strengthen its ranks and force the rest of the world to pay attention to it. Debate about the "legitimacy" of such groups may continue forever, but they care little about how they are described while they use media to capture the spotlight and advance toward their goals.

Beyond the machinations of organizations, benign and not, new media enable issues to percolate rapidly toward the upper reaches of the public's agenda. The acceleration of the gay marriage movement in the United States was an example of this. The shift in attitude may have been partly generational, but the speed at which support built for legislative and judicial action was attributable to a significant degree to ubiquitous social media conversation and endorsements of the cause. Visibility enhances the legitimacy of an issue, or at least its salience, and implicitly encourages the public to ponder it.

During the next few years, we will see if other issues develop similar momentum: matters related to climate change and access to water; global health initiatives; and topics concerning women, including global access to education and protection from rape during conflict.

All such changes, as matters of both politics and conscience, will require adjustments in diplomatic priorities. The US State Department in 2010 began a formal process to try to keep up with a changing diplomatic environment. The latest iteration of its Quadrennial Diplomacy and Development Review (QDDR) was published in 2015. It reaffirmed the status of development as a principal pillar of US foreign policy and acknowledged the growing significance of non-state actors and the need to build partnerships with them as well as with states. The report cited "civil society, citizen movements, faith leaders, entrepreneurs, and others who share our interests and values." As for strategic priorities, the QDDR reflected the localized turmoil plaguing much of the world, noting the need to combat violent extremism and "prevent and respond to internal conflict, atrocities, and fragility." The report also stressed the need to foster "inclusive economic growth" and "mitigating and adapting to climate change."[3]

These objectives are nicely uncontroversial in their broad sense, but diplomats are likely to find that implementing the policies they require will be challenging. Encouraging "inclusive economic growth," for instance, can collide head-on with "mitigating and adapting to climate change." A diplomat working in a small Global South country might well encounter strong support for the former and little concern about the latter, which may be dismissed as a problem created by the major industrial powers, who should be responsible for fixing it without penalizing those countries aspiring to nascent growth. As for non-state actors, diplomats in the field might have ideas entirely different from those of their remote policy chiefs about which elements of "civil society, citizen movements," and so on are most worthy of partnership.

So, despite all the improvements in communication between Washington and US diplomats in the field, top-down management still struggles for balance with on-site judgment. This is particularly acute because the publics with which diplomats in the field must work can avail themselves of so many information sources and have so many outlets through which they can express their interests, dissatisfaction, and other attitudes. These sometimes cacophonous voices contribute to opinion currents that run strongly through the global public, regardless of the worldview enunciated by the US State Department or other foreign ministries.

To advance their own countries' national interests, diplomats must become more attentive to "public issues" – those that emerge from the swirl of talk and civic action enhanced by the new connectivity. Issues may gain traction even if receiving only lip service from senior officials. Access to an adequate supply of safe water may be one of these issues. For most people in industrialized nations, water security is an abstraction, although prolonged drought in places such as California has begun to awaken publics even in the richest countries. But in places where clean water has long been scarce, and where diseases such as cholera and typhoid flourish, this is a daily life-and-death issue. The difference today is that more people can talk about it, using social media, and they expect to be heard. Diplomats must, as a practical as well as moral imperative, attune their antennae so they can listen and respond to these conversations.

Social media allow discussions about public issues such as this to extend the concentric circles of discourse. These circles traditionally did not reach far: household, immediate family, neighbors, co-workers. Not much of a base to attract notice or mobilize opinion. Diplomats were unlikely to even become aware of the issues involved, much less see a need to formulate a response. Today (and tomorrow), however, as social media access becomes more widespread, these circles will expand considerably. Diplomats will be among those who will need to monitor, and in some cases participate in, such discussions because they can help map a path for effective public diplomacy; in this case, providing water-related assistance. In certain instances, social media may also provide early warning about incipient instability in a country, as was belatedly recognized concerning social media content related to the Arab uprisings of 2011.

Advanced communication technology will also play an ever-larger role in responding to humanitarian emergencies, which, although primarily a moral duty, is also a key element in how a country is viewed by the rest of the world. Among these operations are earthquake rescue efforts, protecting refugees from predatory attacks, supplying food during famine, and other such measures that are within the capabilities of "first world" states. Within a few years, improved mobile technology will be in the hands of most people on the planet, ensuring a stronger flow of information during emergencies as well as at other times. Diplomats will be relied upon as "information first responders," providing reports to and from governments and relief organizations.

Such tasks are far removed from diplomats' duties of years past. But just as new communication technologies involve more people in diplomatic conversation and increase the velocity of the diplomatic process, so too do they expand the scope of the diplomat's role. This leads to an important question: how far do media opportunities extend, and should there be limits to the uses of new media?

## The quest for data

If we accept the idea that new media open the way for greater public involvement in many aspects of policymaking and policy implementation, how can diplomats determine what this "public" is in terms of their attitudes and priorities? How can foreign ministries and their overseas outposts avoid being blindsided by a popular uprising or unanticipated election result? How can they determine if a loud online voice is truly representative – or just loud? And when surprises happen, how should diplomats respond?

The collection of information can be broader and more precise than ever before, thanks to growing technological ability to analyze "big data." Trying to define "big" in this context will only hurt your brain, so it might be best to visualize data as a mountain with a summit that moves ever higher, always out of reach. Moving upward from a base camp several decades ago, data analysts have been able to climb closer to the summit as they process greater and greater chunks of data within reasonable time frames. This involves moving far past gigabytes to terabytes and petabytes and ever upward.

The summit may never be reached, but the rate of climb is accelerating and huge amounts of data are becoming more manageable, and thus more valuable. An example from domestic politics: Barack Obama's 2012 reelection campaign employed 100 analytics experts who developed a system in which individual voters' interests could be tracked and could elicit personalized contact from the campaign. This replaced the previous practice of identifying wide swathes of the electorate – labor union members, for instance – and targeting them with campaign material that had to be extremely general in its content. It was impractical to be more precise; even when data about Jane Smith's personal interests were available, there was no way to analyze it along with similar data from millions of other workers and generate personalized responses. By 2012, that problem had been resolved, at least to the point at which Ms. Smith's interests could be addressed directly by the Obama team.[4]

With varying degrees of difficulty, similarly large amounts of data can be collected throughout the world, and can be analyzed with unprecedented speed and thoroughness. What, however, are diplomats to do with this information? The answer to that may lead to a significant expansion of diplomats' responsibilities that will require a new set of sophisticated job skills. Embassies may become frontline administrators of big data collection, working with – and perhaps sometimes creating – local public opinion research firms and sending the information home to the foreign ministry for analysis. Once this process becomes efficiently systematized, foreign policy leadership should have a far better understanding of the populations with which they are dealing, and diplomats in the field will be able to complete their tasks with greater precision.

## Narratives

It is still too early to tell how the public will react once it realizes that it is being so closely analyzed by foreign ministries, political candidates, advertising agencies, and others. There may be pushback in some countries through statutory limits on data collection. But public unhappiness will be irrelevant to some governments. If the Chinese government, for example, wants to collect and study big data about its own citizens and people elsewhere, it will do so (as it presumably is already doing).

Among the products of this enhanced data analysis will be

information to be used in shaping narratives, which are central elements of nations' efforts to portray themselves favorably to global publics. "This is who we are, this is what we believe, and this is what we aspire to"; these are among the pieces of a narrative. Sadly, one of today's best known narratives is based largely on falsehood and betrayal of faith, but it has proven effective. It belongs to the Islamic State.

The social media messaging with which IS has found notable success is not about its beheadings or battlefield conquests, but rather is its call to young people to join in building the caliphate – the Islamic nation – that IS claims to champion. Emphasis is not on wielding a rifle or a sword, but rather on creating a Muslim state in which religion is uncorrupted by Western influences.

IS's online videos include one that shows the organization's fighters playing with their children in a playground; no weapons or violence in sight. Another video depicts a well-equipped pediatric ward in an IS hospital. News reports have stated that among the Western Muslims joining IS in Syria have been young physicians and medical students. There was nothing in the background of these women and men to suggest an affinity for violence. The narrative that helped convince them was not "Come kill," but "Come create."

The call to help build a new state that is at the heart of such messages is not unique to IS. In mid-nineteenth-century America, the narrative of "manifest destiny" inspired the advice "Go west, young man, and grow up with the country." The chance to be a pioneer always piques interest that when nurtured, as IS has done through its online presence, can lead to people setting out on what promises to be a constructive adventure. Such messaging has proved particularly effective among young Arabs in the Middle

East and elsewhere who see their lives as being without hope – no job, no stable home, and no respect shown to their religion or themselves. As in centuries past, these are people willing to take risks to find what they hope will be better lives.

The IS narrative glitters. It is, however, built on lies, and those who respond to the "build the caliphate" message will likely find themselves sucked into the real work of IS: murder, rape, enslavement. To those who saw only IS's bloody activities, as presented in news reports, the group's evil is self-evident. But IS's shrewdness in using social media to define itself as a positive enterprise must not be underestimated.

Exposing the true IS requires a counter-narrative that debunks the caliphate-building message. That can best be done by taking it on directly. Although anti-IS messaging should make clear that IS's bloodlust betrays the *ummah* – the global Muslim community – it must also confront the IS premise that Islam is best served when Muslims isolate themselves from the rest of the world, which is what the IS caliphate promises.

The effectiveness of the IS narrative underscores the complexities of intellectual combat on social media. For some, the basic weaponry includes an Orwellian approach to truth, the persistence and fundamental skills needed to maintain a highly visible online presence, a shrewd understanding of the psychology of the intended audience, and, most importantly, the ability to translate a political mission into a compelling story.

IS is not alone in its ability to do this. It is the descendant of the Goebbels-orchestrated Nazi propaganda campaigns of the 1930s and has present-day kinship with such self-justifying arguments as those presented by Russia about its adventurism in Ukraine. Every nation and non-state actor has a narrative of one kind or another (and individuals do, as well). As disgusting as IS is in so many ways, it should be studied because its narrative has done what its creators want it to do, which is attract impressionable young Muslims. It may be just a matter of time before the realities of IS catch up with its deceptive messaging, and the counter-narratives presented by the anti-IS coalition become coherent enough to become more convincing.

Diplomats are essential in delivering their own nations' narratives and countering those that are contrary to their nations' interests. Social media are seen as indispensable in this and are redefining standards for outreach. British diplomat Tom Fletcher, who has served as ambassador to Lebanon, noted, "We judge that it is not now worth doing a speech unless it is reaching, via social media, over one thousand people."[5]

As is the case with almost all media-oriented foreign policy initiatives, whether on the micro or macro scale, narratives take us once again into the realm of public diplomacy. If IS can reach publics effectively, its opponents must do the same. The worst thing that can happen is to surrender the domain of narrative to "the bad guys."

Narratives that are intrinsically manipulative will not endure. When false, they will be undermined by truth; when hateful, they will be conquered by decency. This might take a while; a well-constructed narrative can sustain attacks, but none is impregnable. More and more, diplomats will find themselves engaged in this process: presenting narratives for their own country, and attacking those from hostile sources.

For a narrative to be effective, it must have substance behind it. Mere glibness will not suffice, and even respected world leaders will be held to account if their promises are not backed up by solid policy. Were this not the case, governments could simply hire novelists or Hollywood screenwriters to invent narratives with audience appeal. But not even Harry Potter can transform foreign policy into something it isn't. Barack Obama, whose skills might not have matched those of Harry Potter, discovered this when he attempted, in 2009, to present a new narrative about America's relationship with the Muslim world. He delivered a beautifully written speech in Cairo, in which he said, among other things, "The situation for the Palestinian people is intolerable. And America will not turn our backs on the legitimate Palestinian aspiration for dignity, opportunity, and a state of their own."[6] This apparent commitment was at the heart of a new US narrative and it was well received in the Arab and larger Muslim community. But within a short time, this same community came to realize that Obama's words signaled no real change in US policy. The narrative collapsed, and so did the surge in popularity that Obama and the United States briefly enjoyed within this constituency.

The public's credulity extends only so far. This makes the success of the IS narrative mysterious, because IS social media dispatches must compete against coverage by traditional news media of the horrific crimes IS commits. At some point, presumably, the concerted anti-IS efforts on traditional and social media will help reduce the organization's audience to a lunatic fringe and shrink the flow of recruits traveling into Syria and Iraq. But for those who study the content and means of delivery of narratives, IS provides a sad but useful example of success.

With diverse narratives and so much other information surging into the public domain, diplomats must sometimes feel they are swatting at flies as they try to keep on track with their duties. This, however, is the new information environment within which diplomacy must now be conducted. Speed and intensity will only increase as the online population leaves its stationary computers behind and increases its reliance on mobile devices. Stimuli for messaging will multiply, as online information will be supplemented by "what I heard on the bus" triggering a quick text or tweet, which in turn may ignite a multiplier effect as recipients retransmit the information.

Some basic statistics illustrate the breadth of these changes.[7] As of early 2015, the global population totaled about 7.2 billion. Of these:

- 3 billion were active internet users (up 21 percent from the previous year).
- 3.6 billion were unique mobile users.
- Of 2.1 billion active social media accounts, 1.7 billion were on mobile devices.

To cite India, with a population of 1.28 billion, as an example, 27 percent of web page views were on desktops or laptops, and 72 percent were on mobile phones. In China, with a population of 1.37 billion, there are 1.3 billion mobile connections, and of 629 million active social media accounts, 506 million are mobile.

It is possible to wallow in statistics indefinitely, but the numbers cited here serve at the very least to indicate the scope of a phenomenon that was practically nonexistent just a few years ago. This is the crowded, bustling environment in which diplomats must work.

## Diplomacy in the new global community

The diplomacy of major powers receives the most attention, which is fitting because they can do the most good or create the most havoc. But the doors to what used to be a closed club have been pushed at least partly open by the forces of globalization. Countries that used to be ignored now receive attention not only because of their recently accessed natural resources, which other states covet, but also because they can use new media tools to call attention to their accomplishments and needs. The landscape of power is gradually flattening.

This leads to emerging countries having greater interest in interacting with other states. While once isolation was either self-imposed or the result of lack of concern by others, such cocoons are now being shed. One example: Ethiopia, best known by much of the world for its wars and famines, is among those nations becoming more outward-looking. When it convened its diplomatic representatives – ambassadors, consuls, and others – in Addis Ababa in 2015, one of the principal themes was finding new ways to use diplomatic tools to augment development and democratization efforts, and expand existing emphasis on technology transfers, trade, and investment. With a smaller foreign policy establishment than those of many countries, Ethiopia counts on its diplomats to help shape policy as well as execute it. One example cited at the meeting in Addis Ababa was the responsibility of diplomats to determine what kinds of assistance Ethiopia needs and what it has done with assistance when given. Also noted at the sessions was training for diplomats in economic diplomacy and in using digital media in their jobs.[8]

Not too many years ago, Ethiopia's leaders would not have

been contemplating such matters. The international community was looked to for emergency aid plus ongoing help from the United Nations and NGOs, and little else. Ethiopia today, however, is no longer a supplicant nation. It is ratcheting up its international involvement, reaching a level of diplomatic self-sufficiency. Ethiopia's economy and civil society are still under construction, but its diplomatic efforts create balance between its domestic tasks and its broader ambitions.

## Manipulating social media

Much of the work of diplomats involves gathering and evaluating information. They constantly take the pulse of global publics so policymakers may be fully informed. (Intelligence agencies' operatives do similar work, although much of their information-gathering presumably includes different methods than those diplomats use.) With so much information in plain view, analyzing the public opinion it reflects may seem an easy task. The number of retweets, for example, would seem a useful measure of the popularity of that particular message.

But the age of innocence for social media did not last long. Those retweets might be the work of "trolls" – robotic computer programs (or robotic humans) that amplify particular messages, often at the behest of a government. Russia, for one, expends considerable effort on this kind of manipulation of social media. Not only will Russian officials concoct, for example, a conspiracy theory about the shooting down over Ukraine of a Malaysia Airlines passenger jet in 2014, it will unleash its mechanical and human trolls to ensure that its message – perhaps including photoshopped images – pervades social media. This message will find believers in Russia, eastern Ukraine, and elsewhere, and if they retweet or respond, the trolls will push their messages as well to a larger audience. This effort may drown out individual voices on social media who do not avail themselves of deceptive measures.[9]

What this means for diplomats is that the enticing river of open source information will sometimes be polluted. Much social media content is neatly quantifiable, but as the work of trolls shows, the numbers can easily be skewed and so their allure should be resisted. The next step will be to further develop tools that can detect differences between genuine "grassroots" opinion and artificial, "astroturf" content. Until those tools are available, "sentiment analysis" that relies on social media will be an inexact science.

## Refugees and new media

Diplomats are among those who must deal with the always difficult challenges presented by global migration. Natural disasters and wars can trigger mass movements of people willing to take enormous risks to escape their dangerous circumstances. Individual governments and international organizations work together to address the migrants' needs while being mindful of their own interests. An influx of migrants into a relatively poor country can add an economic catastrophe on top of the problems that drove the migrants away from their homelands.

The numbers are huge. During the first six months of 2015, more than 300,000 people crossed the Mediterranean Sea looking for refuge, landing primarily in Greece and Italy. This was an increase of approximately 50 percent from the number on the same routes during all of 2014. Meanwhile, Turkey had received about two million refugees, most fleeing the war in Syria and Iraq, and Jordan – by no means a wealthy country – was hosting nearly a million refugees from the same conflict. The United Nations assisted the government of Jordan in aiding these refugees.[10]

Jordan was merely a temporary stop for refugees who, once they decided that conditions in their homeland would prevent a return anytime soon, began to make their way toward Western Europe in the hope of finding a job and decent living conditions. In August 2015, 3,000 refugees on this trek crossed from Greece into Macedonia every day.

During their journeys, many refugees rely heavily on social media, and in so doing they provide an example of the expanding effects of new media tools. Migrants use smartphone maps, global positioning apps, messaging applications such as WhatsApp, and other connections to plot their journeys, stay in touch with distant family members, keep informed about locations of border guards, crossing points, and predatory gangs, and generally diminish the isolation of migrant life. These tools have also reduced the need to rely on illegal traffickers, because Facebook sites and other online content give them enough information to travel independently. To assist in this process, the United Nations High Commissioner for Refugees distributed 33,000 SIM cards to refugees in Jordan and gave away more than 85,000 solar lanterns that can be used to charge mobile phones.[11]

The refugees' experience is relevant to the work of diplomats because social media allow governments to connect directly with migrants who have arrived in their country or who are heading in their direction. Given the bloody conditions in countries such as Syria, Iraq, and Libya, the movement of large numbers of refugees is likely to continue, and the states they are passing through or where they are ending their journeys will engage in diplomacy to address problems of burden-sharing. Providing food and shelter and ensuring security require multinational efforts, and the diplomats who must deal with these matters can inform themselves about facts on the ground and shape their policies by using the same tools the migrants rely on.

This case shows how new media are changing the way the world works, bridging the tasks of diplomacy to the circumstances of global publics. This is the environment to which diplomacy must adjust.

## Mobilization around the Iran deal

Closer to traditional diplomatic tasks was the debate, primarily in the United States, about the Joint Comprehensive Plan of Action – the Iran nuclear deal of 2015. The partisan acrimony surrounding debate about the deal is described earlier in this book, and the use of social media in announcing the deal is described earlier in this chapter. As the debate about the deal proceeded, social media continued to play a significant role.

It seemed as if everyone wanted to join in, at the very least posting news articles they agreed with on Facebook or tweeting them to the world. Iranian Foreign Minister Javad Zarif was among those who tweeted frequently (in English, @JZarif) in support of the agreement. Established special interest groups used social media to deliver their messages, but perhaps most notable were the efforts of new, ad hoc groups that capitalized on this inexpensive way to reach millions and to organize events around the world. On August 15, 2015, #SupportIranDeal held rallies in more than 100 cities worldwide: Washington, DC, Auckland, Vienna, and Kampala among them. These all were anchored in the virtual world, relying on Facebook, Twitter, YouTube, and other new media. The "organization" was initiated by Iranians (inside Iran and elsewhere) who were tired of their country being sanctioned and ostracized by much of the world. But it didn't matter where the movement originated. The media tools at the organizers' disposal allowed them to connect from anywhere with supporters anywhere.

This was a more sophisticated version of what had been seen four years earlier during the 2011 Arab rebellions, when social media, along with satellite television, were important in organizing large, anti-government demonstrations. By 2015 the technology was better and reached more people (and these demonstrations did not take place in the dangerous environments of Cairo and other Arab cities where governments cracked down on protestors).

Most significant about this activism is how it may affect the outcome of diplomacy. Almost a century earlier, Woodrow Wilson emerged from the diplomatic maneuvering that produced the Treaty of Versailles and tried to galvanize public support for ratifying the treaty and its League of Nations by traveling across the United States, giving speeches in a one-man missionary effort. The trip, by railroad, covered 8,000 miles in 22 days, and its exhausting pace destroyed the president's health. Eventually, the Senate defeated the treaty.

But how else was Wilson to make his case? He could not rely on even supportive newspapers to match his eloquence and passion. To connect with the American public, he had to do so in person. Meanwhile, the Europeans whose lives would be most affected by the treaty had no way to make themselves heard in the

American political debate. Wilson's dream of a world at peace and an enforcement mechanism to ensure that peace was unable to spur a truly global movement; the connectivity needed for international publics to cooperate did not exist.

The lessons of the 2015 debate about Iran, at least for our purposes, are not about the merits of the agreement but rather are illustrative of how new media enhance the empowerment of the global public. Mass demonstrations are not new; opponents of the Vietnam War during the 1960s and 1970s, and supporters of a nuclear weapons freeze during the early 1980s, were able to mobilize hundreds of thousands of supporters around the world. But their ability to deliver their messages to larger publics was principally dependent on the news media. There were no forums such as YouTube or Facebook available to make a movement's case without being filtered by news organizations. It was far easier for governments to ride out the storms of protest because, in terms of information dissemination, the movements had limited venues in which they could try to convince the public of the merits of their cause.

Diplomats and others in government who opposed a movement's message could rely on "intellectual containment" imposed by limited communication. This restricted the reach and clout of external political forces, whether in their home countries or elsewhere. As forceful as citizen movements could sometimes become, their leaders often found themselves "preaching to the choir," rather than significantly expanding their popular base.

Today, however, the reach of proselytizers is almost limitless. With messages moving so quickly and pervasively, diplomats cannot reasonably hope that a political movement will soon evaporate or that its reach will be limited. The Iran agreement debate showed that public lobbying, if well organized, can substantially influence business that once was largely the province of diplomats.

Looking ahead, diplomats must find ways to become more integral parts of this process. Optimists would say "cooperate," while cynics would favor "co-opt." Whatever the intent of the participants, the future of diplomacy will be increasingly democratized, with new media providing the principal tools for change.

## The future and the past

Harold Nicolson wrote that it was "only after the Congress of Vienna in 1815 that the diplomatic service was recognized as a profession distinct from that of the statesman or politician, or that it acquired, in definite form, its own rules, conventions, and prescriptions."[12]

During the intervening two centuries, diplomats have had their share of triumphs and failures. The profession's aristocratic sheen has largely worn off, although the Oxbridge-Ivy League axis is still evident in high places. Until just a few years ago, a rogues' gallery of Western diplomats' photos would have had a bland repetitiveness: Caucasian men, expensively dressed, looking wise and resolute. That has certainly changed; in the United States, of the five most recent secretaries of state (as of mid-2015), two have been African American and three have been women.

And yet, has the essence of diplomacy really changed very much? In a 1961 speech, George F. Kennan said that the classic function of diplomacy is "to effect the communication between one's own government and other governments or individuals abroad, and to do this with maximum accuracy, imagination, tact, and good sense." Kennan had a sense of the changing scope of this work, adding that "the conduct of foreign policy rests today on an exercise in understanding, truly staggering in its dimension – understanding not just of the minds of a few monarchs or prime ministers, but understanding of the minds and emotions and necessities of entire peoples."[13]

Between those two passages from Kennan's speech is a bridge connecting diplomacy's past, present, and future. The focus on governments has expanded to include "entire peoples" – the publics who today have the means and, increasingly, the desire to learn about and participate in matters that were once wholly within the domain of the diplomat. Understanding these publics requires close attention to listening, enhanced by political empathy, a skill-set that most old-style diplomats would not recognize.

During the latter part of the twentieth century, all those involved in foreign policy came to understand the power of television and how it affected their work. As we move farther into this new century, the role of social media takes on similar importance. As a tool to spread information (and disinformation), unite communities of interest, and mobilize political actors, social media possess unprecedented speed and reach, both of which will continue to grow.

Standing alone, technological wizardry – no matter how awe-inspiring – means little. Its effects depend on how it is used and what the motivations are of those who use it. In all this, the diplomat still matters. She or he will confront daunting challenges: conflicts that erupt with distressing frequency and require adroit peacemaking; pandemics that must be countered by rapid, coordinated responses from governments and NGOs; climate change and other environmental matters that can be addressed only through global cooperation; refugee flows that sweep across borders and need compassionate multinational attention. Diplomats should look upon their new array of media-related tools as providing the opportunity to fully integrate their work with the lives of the people they seek to reach and serve.

In this new era, diplomacy will not become obsolete. It will be essential in building a peaceful, prosperous, healthy world. Its traditions will be enhanced by new practices. For diplomacy, a promising future awaits.

# Notes

## 1 Introduction

1 Harold Nicolson, *Diplomacy*, 2nd edn. (London: Oxford University Press, 1950), 168.

## Chapter 1 Open Diplomacy

1 Enrique de Argaez, "Facebook Daily Active Users," *Internet World Stats News*, No. 84, May 7, 2015.
2 https://about.twitter.com/company.
3 http://www.google.com/loon/.
4 Taylor Owen, *Disruptive Power: The Crisis of the State in the Digital Age* (New York: Oxford University Press, 2015), 158.
5 Andreas Sandre, *Digital Diplomacy: Conversations on Innovation in Foreign Policy* (Lanham, MD: Rowman & Littlefield, 2015), 100.
6 David Paul Nickles, *Under the Wire: How the Telegraph Changed Diplomacy* (Cambridge, MA: Harvard University Press, 2003), 77, 78, 86.

7 Paul W. White, *News on the Air* (New York: Harcourt Brace, 1947), 31. See also, Philip Seib, *Broadcasts from the Blitz: How Edward R. Murrow Helped Lead America into War* (Dulles, VA: Potomac Books, 2006), 1–47.

8 Archibald MacLeish, "A Superstition Is Destroyed," in "In Honor of a Man and an Ideal: Three Talks on Freedom," CBS (privately printed booklet), December 2, 1941, 6–7.

9 George F. Kennan, *At a Century's Ending: Reflections 1982–1995* (New York. W.W. Norton, 1996), 297.

10 Walter Goodman, "The Images that Haunt Washington," *New York Times*, May 5, 1991.

11 Walter Goodman, "Silent Partner Emerging in Policy Councils: TV," *New York Times*, March 6, 1993.

12 Mary Ann Watson, *The Expanding Vista* (New York: Oxford University Press, 1990), 223.

13 Elmer Lower, "A Television Network Gathers the News," in Bradley S. Greenberg and Edwin D. Parker (eds.), *The Kennedy Assassination and the American Public* (Stanford, CA: Stanford University Press, 1965), 72.

14 Henry Kissinger, *World Order* (New York: Penguin Press, 2014), 357.

15 Sandre, *Digital Diplomacy*, 236, 258, 263.

16 Ibid., 19, 117.

17 Peter Boyer, "Famine in Ethiopia," *Washington Journalism Review*, January 1985, 19.

18 Owen, *Disruptive Power*, 9.

19 Sandre, *Digital Diplomacy*, 86.

20 Owen, *Disruptive Power*, 150.

### Chapter 2 The Rise of Public Diplomacy

1 http://www.britishcouncil.org/organisation/history.

2 Geoffrey Wiseman, "Conclusion," in Geoffrey Wiseman (ed.), *Isolate or Engage: Adversarial States, U.S. Foreign Policy, and Public Diplomacy* (Stanford, CA: Stanford University Press, 2015), 298.

3 R. S. Zaharna, "From Pinstripes to Tweets," *Cairo Review* 16, Winter 2015, 103.

4 *Another U.S. Deficit: China and America – Public Diplomacy in the Age of the Internet*, Minority Staff Report. Committee on Foreign Relations, United States Senate, February 15, 2011, 2. Available at: http://www.foreign.senate.gov/imo/media/doc/ S%20Prt%20Another%20US%20Deficit%20China%20and% 20America%20Public%20Diplomacy%20in%20the%20Age% 20of%20the%20Internet%2003042011.pdf.

5 David Shambaugh, "China's Soft-Power Push," *Foreign Affairs*, vol. 94, no. 4, July–August 2015, 105.

6 Will Wachter, "The Language of Chinese Soft Power in the U.S.," *Asia Times Online*, May 24, 2007.

7 "On Partnerships with Foreign Governments: The Case of Confucius Institutes," American Association of University Professors, June 2014. Available at: http://www.aaup.org/ report/confucius-institutes.

8 Leon Aron, "Putinformation," *Weekly Standard*, August 10, 2015, 23.

9 Ibid.

10 Ibid.

11 "Aux Armes, Journalistes!," *Economist*, March 21, 2015, 49.

12 Connie Bruck, "Friends of Israel," *The New Yorker*, September 1, 2014.

13 Theodore C. Sorensen (ed.), *"Let the Word Go Forth": The Speeches, Statements and Writings of John F. Kennedy* (New York: Dell/Laurel, 1991), 60.

14 http://www.peacecorps.gov/about/fastfacts/.

15 Charles Kenny, "Corps Concerns," *Foreign Policy*, February 22, 2011. Available at: http://foreignpolicy.com/2011/02/22/ corps-concerns/.

16 "U.S. Investment in Entrepreneurship," White House fact sheet, July 25, 2015. Available at: https://www.whitehouse. gov/the-press-office/2015/07/25/fact-sheet-us-investment- entrepreneurship.

17 "Twiplomacy Study 2015." Available at: http://twiplomacy. com/blog/twiplomacy-study-2015/.

18 Bradley Hope, "Spy Software Gets a Second Life on Wall Street," *Wall Street Journal*, August 3, 2015.

19 Lawrence Wright, *The Looming Tower* (New York: Knopf, 2006), 23.

20 Robert Banks, *A Resource Guide to Public Diplomacy Evaluation* (Los Angeles, CA: Figueroa Press, 2011), 11.

## Chapter 3 States and Non-States

1 Joseph S. Nye, Jr., *Is the American Century Over?* (Cambridge: Polity, 2015), 112.

2 Ibid., 105.

3 Ben Hubbard, "Offering Services, ISIS Digs In Deeper in Seized Territories," *New York Times*, June 17, 2015.

4 Tim Arango, "ISIS Transforming into Functioning State that Uses Terror as Tool," *New York Times*, July 21, 2015.

5 Stephen M. Walt, "What Should We Do if the Islamic State Wins? Live With It," *Foreign Policy*, June 10, 2015. Available at: http://foreignpolicy.com/2015/06/10/what-should-we-do-if-isis-islamic-state-wins-containment/.

6 Adam Taylor, "Why the BBC Said No When David Cameron Asked It To Stop Using the Term Islamic State," *Washington Post*, July 2, 2015.

7 Data provided by Doctors Without Borders (United States).

8 Ivo Daalder, "A New Global Order of Cities," *Financial Times*, May 26, 2015.

9 Rogier van der Pluijm and Jan Melissen, *City Diplomacy: The Expanding Role of Cities in International Politics* (The Hague: Clingendael, Netherlands Institute of International Relations, 2007), 21.

10 David Duckenfield, "From Local to Global: Why Diplomacy Matters," *DipNote*, US Department of State, October 26, 2015. Available at: Blogs.state.gov/stories/2015/10/26/local-global-why-diplomacy-matters.

11 www.mega-cities.net.

12 Barry Pavel, Peter Engelke, and Alex Ward, *Dynamic Stability: U.S. Strategy for a World in Transition*, Atlantic Council Strategy Paper, No. 1, 13. Available at: http://www.atlantic-council.org/images/publications/DynamicStabilityStrategy Paper_04202015_WEB.pdf.

13 https://en.wikipedia.org/wiki/Overseas_Pakistani.

14 N. K. Singh, "Diaspora Could Become Vehicle of India's Soft Power," *Hindustan Times* (New Delhi), August 31, 2015. Available at: http://www.hindustantimes.com/analysis/india -s-global-diaspora-could-become-a-key-component-of-soft-power/article1-1385866.aspx.

15 Deborah L. Trent, "Public-Private Partnership Programs with U.S.-Based Diasporas," *CPD Blog*, July 16, 2015. Available at: http://uscpublicdiplomacy.org/blog/public-private-partner ship-programs-us-based-diasporas.

16 Josh Richardson, "The Somali Diaspora: A Key Counterterrorism Ally," Combating Terrorism Center at West Point, July 1, 2011. Available at: https://www.ctc.usma.edu/ posts/the-somali-diaspora-a-key-counterterrorism-ally.

17 Susan J. Matt, "The New Globalist Is Homesick," *New York Times*, March 21, 2012.

18 Christina Slade, *Watching Arabic Television in Europe* (Basingstoke: Palgrave Macmillan, 2014), 13.

19 Matilda Andersson, Marie Gillespie, and Hugh Mackay, "Mapping Digital Diasporas @ BBC World Service: Users and Uses of the Persian and Arabic Websites," *Middle East Journal of Culture and Communication*, vol. 3, 2010, 256–7, 270.

20 Andersson, Gillespie, and Mackay, "Mapping Digital Diasporas," 276.

21 Heather Kelly, "Facebook Rainbow Profiles Used by 26 Million," *CNN Money*, June 29, 2015. Available at: http://money.cnn. com/2015/06/29/technology/facebook-rainbow-profile/.

22 Robert D. Kaplan, "The Art of Avoiding War," *The Atlantic*, June 2015, 32–3.

23  Huston Smith, *The Illustrated World's Religions* (San Francisco, CA: HarperCollins, 1994), 13.

24  Barry Rubin, "Religion and International Affairs," in Dennis R. Hoover and Douglas M. Johnston (eds.), *Religion and Foreign Affairs* (Waco, TX: Baylor University Press, 2012), 521.

25  Ben Hubbard and Mayy El Sheikh, "WikiLeaks Shows a Saudi Obsession with Iran," *New York Times*, July 17, 2015.

26  @Pontifex, July 2, 2015.

27  Madeleine Albright, *The Mighty and the Almighty* (New York: Harper Perennial, 2007), 73.

28  Ibid., 67, 78.

## Chapter 4  Staying on Track

1  Michael Binyon, "Diplomas in Diplomacy," *World Today*, vol. 71, no. 4, August–September 2015, 42.

2  http://www.gpo.gov/fdsys/pkg/GPO-NARA-WSPF-NIXON-GRAND-JURY-RECORDS/pdf/GPO-NARA-WSPF-NIXON-GRAND-JURY-RECORDS-19.pdf, pp. 21-A, 25.

3  https://www.youtube.com/watch?v=7EFMHtmNHbg.

4  Foreign Service Act of 1980 (22 USC 3944), Section 304, http://www.afsa.org/foreign-service-act-1980.

5  David Rothkopf, *National Insecurity* (New York: PublicAffairs, 2014), 207.

6  Robert Hastings, "Strategic Communication: A Department of Defense Perspective," August 20, 2013. Available at: http://www.slideshare.net/RobertTHastings/strategic-communication-a-department-of-d.

7  http://www.pepfar.gov/funding/results/index.htm.

8  Christopher Meyer, "Being a Good Diplomat Requires More than Ferrero Rocher," *The Telegraph*, February 12, 2015. Available at: http://www.telegraph.co.uk/news/worldnews/11407064/Being-a-good-diplomat-takes-more-than-Ferrero-Rocher.html.

9  http://www.state.gov/m/fsi/.

## Chapter 5 Shaping Diplomacy's Future

1 Ilan Manor, "The Framing of #IranDeal on Digital Diplomacy Channels," *Exploring Digital Diplomacy*, July 14, 2015. Available at: http://digdipblog.com/2015/07/14/the-framing-of-irandeal-on-digital-diplomacy-channels/.

2 Lawrence Wright, *Thirteen Days in September* (New York: Knopf, 2014), xiv.

3 http://www.state.gov/s/dmr/qddr/2015/.

4 Andrew Lampitt, "The Real Story of How Big Data Analytics Helped Obama Win," *InfoWorld*, February 14, 2013. Available at: http://www.infoworld.com/article/2613587/big-data/the-real-story-of-how-big-data-analytics-helped-obama-win.html.

5 Sandre, *Digital Diplomacy*, xii.

6 https://www.whitehouse.gov/the-press-office/remarks-president-cairo-university-6-04-09.

7 http://wearesocial.net/blog/2015/01/digital-social-mobile-worldwide-2015/.

8 Mulualem Denbegna, "Ethiopian Diplomats' Role in Nation and Image Building," *Ethiopian Herald* (Addis Ababa), August 14, 2015.

9 Aliya Sternstein, "U.S. Intelligence Community Keys in on the Russian 'Troll Army' Manipulating Social Media," *Nextgov*, August 17, 2015. Available at: http://www.nextgov.com/defense/2015/08/us-intelligence-community-keys-russian-troll-army-manipulating-social-media/119158/.

10 http://www.unhcr.org/cgi-bin/texis/vtx/page?page=49e486566&submit=GO.

11 Matthew Brunwasser, "A 21st-Century Migrant's Essentials: Food, Shelter, Smartphone," *New York Times*, August 26, 2015.

12 Nicolson, *Diplomacy*, 28.

13 George F. Kennan, "Diplomacy as a Profession," speech to the American Foreign Service Association, Washington, DC, March 30, 1961; republished in *Foreign Service Journal*, July/August 2015. http://www.afsa.org/george-kennan-diplomacy-profession.

# Index